Absence

amongst

Abundance

Absence amongst Abundance: Health Inequity and Homelessness in Canada

Authors

Kanish Baskaran, Nicholas Hamzea, Annie Li, Sahir Dhalla, Darla Chloe Daniva, Margarita Liubetskaya, Mohathir Sheikh, Sidra Bharmal, Mariyam Sardar, Cassandra Van Drunen, Angelin Valancia Thipahar, Austin Mardon, Catherine Mardon

Editors

Kanish Baskaran

Naiya Patel

Copyright © 2021 by Austin Mardon

All rights reserved. This book or any portion thereof may not be reproduced or used in any manner whatsoever without the express written permission of the publisher except for the use of brief quotations in a book review or scholarly journal.

First Printing: 2021

Cover Design and typeset by Clare Dalton

Chapter title font: Accanthis ADF Std

(Copyright © Arkandis Digital Foundry
under the GNU General Public License V2)

ISBN 978-1-77369-662-1

E-book ISBN 978-1-77369-663-8

Golden Meteorite Press

103 11919 82 St NW

Edmonton, AB T5B 2W3

www.goldenmeteoritepress.com

Contents

Introduction	9
Chapter 1: Homelessness in Canada	11
Chapter 2: Barriers to accessible healthcare	21
Chapter 3: Impact of barriers to accessible healthcare	29
Chapter 4: Root causes of barriers to accessible healthcare	37
Chapter 5: Impact of COVID-19 on the homeless population	47
Chapter 6: Effect of homelessness on hunger and nutrition	55
Chapter 7: Effect of homelessness on infectious diseases	63
Chapter 8: Effect of Homelessness on Sexual and Reproductive Health	71
Chapter 9: Effect of homelessness on chronic illnesses/ diseases and mortality	81
Chapter 10: Effect of homelessness on addiction	91
Chapter 11: Public Initiatives seeking to address barriers to accessible healthcare	101
Conclusion	109
References	111

Introduction

On any given night, over 8,700 people in Toronto are experiencing homelessness, the effects of which have only been exacerbated by the COVID-19 pandemic. While many organizations and individuals are working tirelessly to address different aspects of this crisis, one often overlooked facet are the significant barriers to healthcare faced by this population. This book delves into the health inequities faced by the homeless population, including the different barriers, their root causes and initiatives and policies looking to address this issue.

Chapter 1:

Homelessness in Canada

Kanish Baskaran

Many of us have a mental image of someone who is homeless, typically seen out on the street with a cardboard sign or bouncing about homeless shelters. This image is based on our personal experiences as well as what we've seen and heard from friends, family, and the media. In actuality, homelessness takes many forms, and there is no such thing as a "typical" type of homelessness. This is also not just restricted to the streets of big cities as many think and can impact individuals living anywhere in Canada. This chapter explores homelessness, including an overview of homelessness, risk factors for homelessness, and the prevalence of homelessness in Canada.

What is Homelessness?

The official definition of Homelessness, according to the Canadian Homelessness Research Network, is as follows;

"Homelessness describes the situation of an individual or family without stable, permanent, appropriate housing, or the immediate prospect, means and ability of acquiring it. It is the result of systemic or societal barriers, a lack of affordable and appropriate housing, the individual/household's financial, mental, cognitive, behavioural, or physical challenges, and/or racism and discrimination. Most people do not choose to be homeless, and the experience is generally negative, unpleasant, stressful and distressing." (Gaetz et al., 2012)

A wide range of housing circumstances fall under this definition of homelessness. The following typology have been assigned to better categorize the various housing situations;

1. Unsheltered – living on the streets or in a place not intended for human habitation. This includes (Gaetz, et al., 2013);
    a. People living in public or private spaces without consent or contact (e.g., sidewalks, squares, parks, vacant buildings)

    b. People living in places not intended for permanent human habitation (e.g., cars, garages, attics, closets, tents, and shacks)

2. <u>Emergency Sheltered:</u> staying in overnight emergency shelters designed for people who are homeless. This includes (Gaetz, et al., 2013);
    a. Emergency overnight shelters
    b. Shelters for individuals/families impacted by family violence
    c. Emergency shelters for people fleeing a natural disaster or destruction of accommodation.

3. <u>Provisionally accommodated:</u> people who are homeless whose accommodation is temporary or lacks security of tenure, including interim (or transitional) housing, people living temporarily with others (couch surfing), or living in institutional contexts (hospital, prison) without permanent housing arrangements. This includes (Gaetz, et al., 2013);
    a. Interim housing for those who are homeless
    b. People living temporarily with others but without guarantee of continued residency or immediate prospects for accessing permanent housing
    c. People accessing short term, temporary rental accommodations without security of tenure.
    d. People in institutional care who lack permanent housing arrangements
    e. Accommodation/reception centers for recently arrived immigrants and refugees.

4. <u>At risk of homelessness:</u> people who are not homeless, but whose current economic and/or housing situation is precarious or does not meet public health and safety standards. This includes (Gaetz, et al., 2013);
    a. People at imminent risk of homelessness: Though in some cases, this can be due to individual factors, in most cases, it is the interaction of structural and

individual risk that led to this situation.
   b. Individuals and families who are precariously housed: Many individuals and families face housing affordability problems due to their income, local economy, and local housing market. This makes them prone to homelessness.

Risk factors for homelessness

The road in and out of homelessness is not linear. A wide variety of experiences and factors (both singular and co-occurring) can lead an individual to lose housing. These situations are often the result of an interaction between structural and individual risks. The following are some factors that can lead to homelessness.

Precarious employment
Precarious employment refers to non-standard employment that does not meet basic needs, is poorly paid, part time (when full-time work is desired), temporary, and/or insecure and unprotected. A sudden expense or change in cost of living/employment status can disrupt the individual's ability to continue their access to housing (Gaetz et al., 2012) .

Sudden unemployment
This primarily refers to a sudden layoff or dismissal from employment. However, it also includes the factors that prevent an effective recovery, including little to no financial savings/assets, or social support to turn to (Gaetz et al., 2012).

Precarious and inadequate housing
Many individuals at risk of homelessness face severe affordability concerns, either as a result of their income, the local economy, or the lack of affordable housing. In either case, the individual's income is not enough to cover the household's basic shelter and non-shelter costs. This

is not just limited to household income and the physical structure of the home, but also to lack of access to necessary supports, such as schools, clean water, sanitation, and employment (Gaetz et al., 2012). According to Statistics Canada, a household is in core housing need if its housing, "falls below at least one of the adequacy, affordability or suitability, standards and it would have to spend 30% or more of its total before-tax income to pay the median rent of alternative local housing that is acceptable (meets all three housing standards)" (Statistics Canada, 2016)

- Adequate housing is reported by residents as not requiring any major repairs. Housing that is inadequate may have excessive mold, inadequate heating or water supply, significant damage, etc.(Statistics Canada, 2016)
- Affordable dwelling costs less than 30% of total before-tax household income. Those in extreme core housing need to pay 50% or more of their income on housing. It should be noted that the lower the household income, the more onerous this expense becomes. (Statistics Canada, 2016)
- Suitable housing has enough bedrooms for the size and composition of the resident household, according to National Occupancy Standard (NOS) requirements. (Statistics Canada, 2016)

Housing-related supports that are about to be discontinued
The Government of Canada has invested millions into its National Housing Strategy to find permanent housing for the many Canadians that need it (Government of Canada, n.d.). A part of this strategy is to provide additional support crucial towards maintaining a stable household. While beneficial, many of the supports provided are time limited. If such resources are withdrawn but sorely required, individuals/families may have increased risk of re-entering homelessness.

Substance Abuse

A complex relationship exists between substance abuse and homelessness. The potential impacts of substance abuse are numerous, including pharmacological effects that might impact decision-making, deteriorating health, accidental death, and increased chances of sexually risky behaviours (The Homeless Hub, n.d.-d). Although substance abuse rates are disproportionately high amongst the homeless population, it isn't the only explanation for an individual's homelessness (The Homeless Hub, n.d.-d). Many people addicted to substances never experience homelessness, but an individual experiencing housing instability has an increased risk of losing their housing if they use substances. Once on the street, an individual with substance abuse faces insurmountable barriers to obtaining health care, including substance use treatment services and recovery supports (The Homeless Hub, n.d.-d).

Division of Household

Situations where a household is divided (such as separation, divorce, conflicts between caregivers and children, or roommates moving out) can leave the affected individual without the resources to continue living at the current residence or obtain a different place of housing (The Homeless Hub, n.d.-d). These individuals face increased risk of homelessness (Gaetz et al., 2012)

Violence/abuse (or direct fear of) in current housing situations

Violence is often cited as a large contributor to homelessness. This is particularly the case in women, where domestic violence has been found to be the leading cause of homelessness. One study showed that 38% of women reported becoming homeless immediately after separating from their partner (Statistics Canada, 2014). However, like with substance abuse, there is no primary explanation linking violence to homelessness. Rather, it is part of a combination of factors both structural and individual/relational that contribute to homelessness risk (The Homeless Hub, n.d.-b). Some forms of violence include;

- Individuals facing gender/violence
- Children and youth experiencing neglect, physical, sexual, and emotional abuse
- Senior abuse
- Racism, homophobia misogyny and other such discrimination

Prevalence of Homelessness

Mass homelessness in Canada started in the 1980s, following a large disinvestment by government in affordable housing, decreased spending on social supports and shifts in the economy(Gaetz et al., 2016). Today, around 235,000 Canadians experience homelessness in a given year with at least 35,000 Canadians being homeless on a given night. This includes those staying in emergency shelters (14,400), staying in Violence against Women shelters(7350), Unsheltered(2880) and in temporary institutional accommodation (4464)
(The Homeless Hub, n.d.-c).

Distribution of Homelessness in Canada
Historically, the homeless population consisted of older, single men. However, the crisis we see today is much more diverse, with women, families, youth, Indigenous Peoples, newcomers, and LGBTQ2S-identifying individuals emerging as key risk groups within the larger homeless population (Gaetz et al., 2016). The following statistics highlight the diversity of the homeless population today;
- Adults (25 – 49) make up the largest age group of people who are homeless(52%)
- Women make up 27.3% of the homeless population
- Youth unaccompanied by adults make up 18.7% of the homeless population
- Indigenous Peoples are greatly overrepresented amongst homeless shelters, making up 28 – 34% of the sample, while indigenous peoples make up less than 5% of the

general population.
- 2.2% are veterans
- While seniors make up a very small percentage of homeless shelter users (less than 4%), they are the only demographic age groups for whom shelter use has increased in the last ten years.

Hidden Homelessness

In addition to the 35,000 estimated Canadians experiencing homelessness, there may be as many as 50,000 "hidden homeless" Canadians on a given night. This term, colloquially referred to as "couch surfing", is used to refer to individuals who are temporarily staying with friends, relatives, or others since they have nowhere else to live and no immediate prospect of permanent housing. No national level studies have been conducted on hidden homelessness in Canada but a study in Vancouver estimated that 3.5 individuals experienced hidden homelessness for every one person experiencing homelessness (Gaetz, Donaldson, Richter, Gulliver, & Vasko, 2013). This was restricted to just Vancouver and different cities have differences in their ability to support the homeless population(Gaetz, Donaldson, Richter, Gulliver, & Vasko, 2013). Nevertheless, the significance of this issue warrants further research and investigation.

Differentiation of Homelessness

For a large majority of Canadians who become homeless, the experience is rather short. While the median length of stay in an emergency shelter is approximately 50 days, 29% stay only one night (The Homeless Hub, n.d.-c). These individuals are referred to as being Transitionally Homeless – homeless for a short period of time (The Homeless Hub, n.d.-c). People who are chronically homeless (homeless for a long period of time) or episodically homeless (moving in and out of homelessness) are a smaller portion of the overall population (Gaetz, Donaldson, Richter, Gulliver, & Vasko, 2013). Despite this, their experience is much more severe compared to those that are transitionally homeless. They face worse personal struggles, including mental and physical health issues, addictions, legal/justice issues, and discrimination (The Homeless Hub, n.d.-a). Furthermore, despite comprising a small portion of the homeless population, they consume more than half of the resources in the homeless system(The Homeless Hub, n.d.-a). This group is also more likely to experience disastrous health crises which require medical intervention, and have a high level of law enforcement run-ins (The Homeless Hub, n.d.-a). Consequently, it's crucial to differentiate between these groups and those transitionally homeless, both in research and in implementing solutions.

Based on estimates from the total number of individuals experiencing homelessness and using shelters on an annual basis (200,000). The following distribution based on length of homelessness was determined (The Homeless Hub, n.d.-c);
- Those experiencing chronic homelessness: 4000 – 8000
- Those experiencing episodic homelessness: 6000 – 22000
- Those who are transitionally homeless: 176,000 – 188,000

Conclusion

The homeless population is one of the most marginalized and misunderstood sub-populations in Canada. While policy and support advancements have been made that have led to a decrease in individuals experiencing homelessness, the issue continues to impact at least 35,000 Canadians on a given night (The Homeless Hub, n.d.-c). Continuous engagement, paired with individualized support, are necessary if we hope to reduce the prevalence of homelessness in the future.

Chapter 2:

Barriers

to

accessible healthcare

Nicholas Hamzea

Introduction

Although Canada is renowned for its universal healthcare system, it is important to make the distinction between universal and accessible. While many Canadian citizens and permanent residents have easy access to numerous levels of healthcare, the same cannot be said for Canada's homeless population. That is, they face countless barriers at the patient, provider, and system level that prevent them from accessing primary healthcare. As of January 2021, it was reported that over 235,000 people experience homelessness per year in Canada, with 25,000 to 35,000 people experiencing homelessness on any given night (Strobel et al., 2021). This means that on any given day, as many as 35,000 individuals may not be receiving adequate and equal healthcare coverage as a result of being homeless. Moreover, it was found that approximately one in every 6 homeless individuals in Toronto reported having at least one unmet healthcare need, whereas women with dependent children had twice as much difficulty accessing health services in comparison to the general population (Shepherd, 2010). This chapter will outline the various barriers facing the homeless population at each of these three levels, as well as their impact on the individual.

Patient-Level Barriers to Accessible Healthcare

There are many barriers to healthcare at the patient level that can restrict one's ability to receive adequate care. Notably among the homeless population, there are barriers at this level due to lack of patient knowledge and priority setting, as well as a lack of trust between the patient and the provider due to a history of poor service when homeless individuals had sought out primary care at an institution. There are also emotional barriers found at the patient level which prevent homeless patients from accessing care.

Emotional Barriers
Emotions such as fear, stress, and shame may also stand in the way of homeless individuals receiving the care they need. Given the already

stressful nature of their situation, the fear of having a health issue diagnosed may add too much additional stress for them to bear without support (Campbell et al., 2015). Moreover, one interviewed client expressed that the feelings of shame or low self-esteem associated with disclosing that they are homeless to health care providers and other staff members prevents some individuals from seeking out care altogether. This fear and feeling of shame is only further exacerbated by some members of the medical community that discriminate against homeless individuals upon learning about their situation, as will be discussed under the section relating to provider-level barriers to accessible healthcare. Many patients, however, felt that their concerns were being dismissed, and that they were not being properly listened to when voicing their concerns regarding both their physical and mental health (Ramsay et al., 2019). Lastly, some patients have difficulty with authority and may have consequently come to fear those with power over them (Campbell et al., 2015). Unfortunately, the patient-provider relationship in the medical system typically represents exactly this, a relationship with an inherent power dynamic where patients feel as if the doctor has control over them. Along with fear of providers in some situations, some patients have also come to experience a lack of trust in their providers. In addition to personal experiences with authority and having their concerns dismissed, many homeless individuals also have heard stories from friends or families detailing similar experiences. Upon hearing numerous accounts across many people in a similar situation, it becomes apparent to homeless individuals that they are not cared for by the healthcare system which leads to a breakdown of trust in providers as well as the system as a whole.

Patient Knowledge and Priority Setting
As a direct consequence of their past and present situation, homeless individuals often need to prioritize treatment for acute problems over other forms of healthcare such as preventative care (Campbell et al., 2015). This need for prioritization combined with other barriers such as lack of access to primary care and financial barriers decrease the level

of access that homeless individuals have to preventative care which, in turn, increases their need to seek treatment for acute and chronic problems that could have potentially been avoided. In addition, there is also a lack of knowledge within the homeless community regarding prevalent illnesses, which decreases motivation to seek care as they are sometimes not even able to determine that a problem exists.

Provider-Level Barriers to Accessible Healthcare

Environmental Barriers and Discrimination by Providers

The term "environmental barriers" typically refers to the atmosphere created within the clinic as well as the location of the clinic itself, both of which are factors that may deter homeless individuals from seeking healthcare. For example, individuals are less likely to attend a clinic or hospital in an unfamiliar area or where there is increased public and police surveillance and control (Campbell et al., 2015). Clinics that contain features such as security guards in waiting rooms and reception desks for check-in also pose environmental barriers to those wishing to access it. One provider in the study commented on these features, stating that "It is not a physical barrier to you and I, but to the marginalized and homeless, that is a physical barrier and they will sooner walk away than face that barrier so less people go to [the clinic]." Evidently, barriers faced by the homeless population extend far beyond just what the average person may be able to see, and this is all due to the past and present experiences of homeless individuals that place them at an unfair disadvantage along with flaws in the system as well.

However, even making it past the aforementioned environmental barriers and ending up in a clinic or hospital does not mean that the fight for equal access to healthcare is over. Although homeless individuals may overcome the barriers that prevent them from getting into a doctors office, it continues to be an uphill battle as many individuals find themselves facing discrimination within the system by doctors, nurses, or other staff (Campbell et al., 2015). As much as 36% of homeless individuals surveyed reported being discriminated against by a doctor or other staff member at least once in the last year in 2014 (Gulliver, 2014). One patient stated that they had gone to an urgent care center due to significant trouble with their lungs and that the doctor initially admitted him to the hospital. Upon asking for the patient's address, however, the patient stated the name of a shelter after which the doctor had told them that their vitals have come a long way since checking in and that they will be discharged. This is just one of many stories that detail the frequent occurrences of how homeless individuals are treated in the healthcares system, and when so many individuals either have first or second hand experiences such as these, it becomes evident why there is such a lack of trust in providers among the homeless population.

Systems-Level Barriers to Accessible Healthcare

Financial Barriers

Although universal health coverage in Canada covers the cost of a majority of hospital and clinic visits, there are other costs associated with seeking primary care that may act as a barrier which prevents homeless individuals from accessing healthcare. To begin, homeless individuals may not have a reliable way to be transported to the hospital or clinic. Available methods of transport are typically expensive and not found in locations that are easily accessible to homeless individuals. This problem is only further exacerbated by factors such as disabilities and living in a large city such as Toronto or Calgary (Campbell et al., 2015). Moreover, transportation via ambulance typically requires a fee, further adding to the financial barriers. In Ontario, for example, an ambulance ride to the hospital typically incurs a cost of $45 if it is deemed medically necessary by a physician, and $240 if it is deemed not medically necessary (Government of Ontario, n.d.). Although there are some conditions in which individuals may be exempt, some members of the homeless population may not meet the conditions and thus be required to pay if they ever need an ambulance. This can only serve to deter them from using ambulance services, even if they are required. Lastly, even those that do have proof of health insurance may be prescribed or recommended treatments or interventions that are not covered by the healthcare system, making it difficult to adhere to the physician's advice (Ramsay et al., 2019). For example, the patient may be prescribed medications not covered by insurance or recommended that they attend counselling that would require them to pay out of their own pocket. Regardless of whether they are able to afford treatment, however, homeless individuals are still placed at a disadvantage as a result of their socioeconomic status (Gulliver, 2014). A study found that even ina universal healthcare system, where physician compensation is not influenced by patient socioeconomic status (SES), those of a lower SES with chronic health concerns were offered fewer appointments than those of higher SES with less severe health concerns, thus demonstrating that this is in fact a systemic issue that runs far deeper than the individual level. Overall, breaking down the healthcare system demonstrates that for some people, the notion of "free healthcare" is in fact anything but that, and a truly universal healthcare system must begin with being truly free of cost for all those who wish to access it.

Structural Barriers
There are also countless structural barriers at the system-level that interfere with a homeless person's ability to access healthcare. First and foremost, although every citizen has the right to healthcare, many homeless individuals do not have a health card or other proof of health insurance due to it being lost or stolen (Campbell et al., 2015). Since proof of health insurance is required in primary care facilities for your treatment to be covered, many individuals find themselves being unable to consequently seek out primary care despite, on paper, being covered by one of the provincial universal health insurance systems.

Clinic and hospital hours also impact a homeless person's ability to access healthcare (Campbell et al., 2015). Many clinics, for example, may only be open during business hours, and given that many of those part of the homeless communities are considered to be part of the "working poor," they may not be able to afford taking time off work to visit a clinic. While some clinics and many hospital emergency departments are open 24 hours a day, they typically triage patients by urgency of treatment needed, meaning that patients may be waiting multiple hours just to ask a question or discuss a seemingly minor health concern.

Lack of a Primary Care Provider

Primary care providers and family doctors are typically the primary means through which Canadians receive care and access the healthcare system, but this is a barrier to the homeless population (Liu & Hwang, 2021). Homeless individuals typically lack a primary care provider and consequently must rely on acute sources of care such as hospital emergency rooms and emergency clinics (Khandor et al., 2011). In fact, less than half of homeless individuals have a family doctor and homeless individuals are five times more likely to be admitted to the hospital compared to the general population (Hwang, 2001). The impact of this? First, there are significantly higher hospitalization and emergency department visit rates among the homeless population compared to the general population as well as significantly higher readmission rates (Khatana et al., 2020). Not having a primary care provider was strongly associated with increasing duration of homelessness, lack of proof of health insurance coverage and having a chronic medical condition (Khandor et al., 2011). As duration of homelessness increases, for example, individuals may begin to prioritize other needs such as food over seemingly non-urgent medical care such as preventative care, thus leading to an increase in problems down the road. With research showing that having long term access to a care provider is associated with increased preventive care, decreased episodic care at emergency departments and decreased hospital care, it becomes evident that lack of access to a primary care provider can have long-term detrimental effects on those experiencing homelessness.

Conclusion

The overall impact of these barriers is abundantly clear; they break the trust between patient and provider, diminish the level of confidence that homeless individuals have in the healthcare system, and increase the rate of negative health outcomes for the homeless population by preventing access to primary care and allied health services. It becomes abundantly clear that having the right to healthcare as a result of being a Canadian citizen in no way means that the system will provide equal and adequate care. The various barriers faced by the homeless population restrict their ability to access one of their fundamental rights, and a multi-faceted approach must be taken if the multi-level barriers to accessible healthcare among the homeless population are to be addressed.

Chapter 3:

Impact of barriers to accessible healthcare

Annie Li

Introduction

The barriers to accessible healthcare present in the patient, provider, and system levels each uniquely impact the quality of patient care delivered to individuals experiencing homelessness in a negative manner. Often times, the aftermath of these impacts have an adverse effect on the health status of this vulnerable community and can further exacerbate existing barriers. In particular, avoidance of care or not seeking aid for prevalent medical concerns is a widespread occurrence amongst the homeless population that is caused by barriers on all levels, and leads to insufficient care or leaving illnesses undiagnosed. This perpetuates obstacles such as stigma and discrimination which leads to decreased accessibility of these necessary services and support for those in need. That being said, due to a variety of growing barriers that result in inadequate patient care, those that experience homelessness or are vulnerably housed are at an increased risk of death and illness as compared to the general population. This is exemplified by the fact that the mortality of homelessness men aged 18-64 is 2-8 times greater than that of men who are stably housed (Liu and Hwang 2021). As such, it is important to closely examine the barriers to accessible healthcare and the downstream effects that impact the health and well-being of individuals experiencing homelessness.

Stigma and Discrimination

Homeless individuals often fear or face stigma and discrimination from healthcare staff when seeking help at a hospital or clinic (Purkey and MacKenzie 2019). Understandably, the potential for judgement, shame, and mistreatment are driving factors of avoidance for many individuals who are debating whether or not to seek care, and can result in detrimental health effects if the required medical attention is not received. This mistrust in the healthcare system is one of the most prevalent barriers for individuals experiencing homelessness and negatively impacts the community as a whole. Both direct (having lived experience) and indirect (obtaining second-hand information or without personal experience) impacts contribute to the barrier of stigma and discrimination.

Direct Impacts

The experiences of stigma of those with direct encounters are overwhelming evidence of the social barriers that prevent vulnerable individuals from seeking the assistance that they require. Stigma is especially prevalent for individuals who have a history of substance abuse as they are heavily subjected to stereotyping, which can further influence the discrimination they face in healthcare settings (Purkey and MacKenzie 2019). For example, one recounting of a homeless individual's experience describes how the care of someone they knew was diminished after it was revealed that the individual lived in a homeless shelter (Campbell et al. 2015). He was then only given Tylenol for his extreme pain due to unjustified beliefs that stronger painkillers, such as those with codeine, would be distributed and used recreationally (Campbell et al. 2015). In this situation, stigma and discrimination directly impacted the patient's care and may have had deleterious effects on their health upon leaving the centre. Their pain may have worsened, resulting in negative effects on their ability to perform necessary tasks such as walking or sleeping. Additionally, the shame and judgement that they faced may deter the individual from visiting a healthcare centre for medical needs in the future as well. This outcome could result in a plethora of injuries and illnesses going untreated or undiagnosed. Furthermore, not only are there instances in which patient care has been poor for those experiencing homelessness, but examples in which care was withheld altogether are also abundant. Another patient narrated his experiences in an emergency department and how he was discharged without sympathy (Campbell et al. 2015). After being admitted for what had previously been described as urgent trouble in his lungs, he was discharged at three in the morning after he had shared that his address was a homeless shelter (Campbell et al. 2015). In this scenario, not only was the patient not able to seek the appropriate care and treatment for his lungs, but he was discharged in the middle of the night with no means of safety, transportation, or support. Unfortunately, this is not uncommon for individuals experiencing homelessness when they visit a healthcare centre, and they are then sometimes forced to walk home. This, too, could result in negative effects on the patient's health as they are not receiving the care that they need and critical illnesses could be going undiagnosed. These negative experiences are frequently cited as factors that compound the feeling of shame and stigma which ultimately lead to mistrust in the healthcare system, deterring further visits to healthcare centres in times of need.

Additionally, the presence of an advocate often results in "delayed" discrimination of the patient. Although patients are able to request an advocate such as a social services worker to be present with them in the healthcare centre, the judgement and stigma is only delayed until the individual is in the absence of their advocate (Purkey and MacKenzie 2019). The presence of the advocate improved the patients' care and increased the likelihood that they would receive adequate and respectful treatment. However, this dynamic only emphasized the stigma faced by the patient once their advocate had left. Similar to the aforementioned impacts of discrimination on vulnerable individuals, this further increases the reluctancy to seek care which can worsen existing health concerns.

Indirect Impacts

Indirect impacts are also present in cases where individuals do not experience the stigma and discrimination from healthcare providers first-hand. However, even though the individual has not had personal or lived experience, word-of-mouth transmission of others' stories and interactions with healthcare providers can deeply impact mistrust and reluctance to seek medical attention (Purkey and MacKenzie 2019). This further perpetuates the avoidance of care which can have both short and long term consequences for the patient and those around them. Due to the anticipation of judgement, individuals experiencing homeless may decide against visiting a healthcare centre even if they are in pain or need help. Consequently, the condition or injury could worsen and impair the individual's ability to walk, sleep, or eat and exacerbate other health issues. Furthermore, leaving illnesses undiagnosed also has severe implications for the health and well-being of this vulnerable population. Similar to avoiding care, undiagnosed conditions have the potential to rapidly worsen over time and impact other areas of the individual's well-being. While individuals may not have experienced the discrimination themselves, learning of the stories from others instills the anticipation of poor treatment. This fear of stigmatizing experiences, although second-hand, is enough to deter individuals from seeking help, being so grave that it supersedes any medical concerns.

Ultimately, stigma and anticipated stigma against individuals experiencing homelessness is a large factor that has adverse impacts on the health status of this population. This obstacle stands between individuals and their ability to access the medical attention they need. In some cases, individuals will opt to evade seeking help or leave in the middle of their care in order to remove themselves from stigmatizing situations.

Inflexibility of the Healthcare System

Even if individuals are able to work past the concerns of stigma and discrimination, the rigid nature of the healthcare system prevents many who are experiencing homelessness or are vulnerably housed from seeking the appropriate care. It has often been stated that the healthcare system has been designed by the middle class for middle class clients and expects others to conform to the system, rather than tailoring its services to the different needs of patients (Purkey and MacKenzie 2019). These systematic barriers worsen the health status of vulnerable individuals and further lessens the accessibility of medical care. Factors such as government identification, clinic hours, and others are some of the most prominent barriers that impact patient care.

Government Identification

A widespread restriction among individuals experiencing homelessness is the lack of government-issued identification which is vital to accessing healthcare resources (Turnbull, Muckle, and Masters 2007). Among the most important is the absence of a provincial health card, which the individual may not possess for a variety of reasons. If the individual was fleeing an abusive home, was assaulted or attacked, it is possible that they no longer have their health card and therefore do not have proof of coverage from Canada's system of universal health coverage. As a result, many individuals are negatively impacted as they are turned away from care and are unable to utilize medical assistance or other resources. In the city of Toronto alone, approximately 7% of individuals experiencing homelessness stated that they had been refused medical care at least once due to a lack of a health insurance card (Turnbull, Muckle, and Masters 2007). Similarly, individuals who have traveled across provincial borders are also faced with difficulties in accessing healthcare as different provincial health cards may not allow for admittance or treatment in one province (Campbell et al. 2015). Without any means of replacing identification or obtaining the correct identification, many vulnerable individuals are not receiving the treatment they need which can rapidly escalate injuries or leave serious conditions undiagnosed.

Clinic Hours

Another structural barrier that negatively impacts patient care includes the limited clinic hours that are available to the public (Campbell et al. 2015). Clinic hours are often rigid and require patients to take time away from their regular work routine. However, while some individuals who experience homelessness are unemployed, the ones that have jobs are often considered to be part of the "working poor", meaning that they are unable to take time off work. Consequently, these individuals are unable to visit clinics that only operate during regular business hours and either have to delay seeking care or skip seeking care altogether. Smaller clinics are often preferable to going to the emergency room simply due to fewer people and shorter wait times to receive care, but an inability to access medical services prevents individuals from getting the help they need. Moreover, healthcare centres that are open twenty-four hours a day, such as hospital emergency departments or overnight clinics, have a larger influx of patients and therefore triage according to the level of urgency. This means that individuals may need to wait hours into the night for a simple question or consultation. This, too, discourages many from paying a clinic visit which leaves health concerns to worsen over time without the proper medical attention.

Other

One of the biggest barriers experienced on an individual scale for homeless persons includes the variety of competing priorities that must be considered in a person's daily life (Liu and Hwang 2021). Often times, securing necessities such as food, water, and shelter take precedence over seeking healthcare and can once again lead to individuals not receiving treatment. Additionally, hospitals and healthcare centres exhibit a lack of flexibility for patients who may be late or miss appointments while managing these contending priorities (Purkey and MacKenzie 2019). Attempts to avoid stigmatizing situations, as aforementioned, also tends to take priority over the need for medical attention for many individuals.

Additionally, the healthcare system is unforgiving when it comes to the lack of education and availability of schooling among vulnerable individuals (Campbell et al. 2015). Not only are there already an abundance of obstacles in place that hinder a patient's ability and accessibility to care, but insufficient knowledge further compounds the negative impacts on patient health. Some individuals may be less aware of illnesses and injuries which may prevent them from noticing potential problems and therefore result in an absence of motivation to seek care. As well, the lack of education may render vulnerable individuals ill-equipped to advocate for themselves in situations where sympathy has been replaced by stigma. Together, these factors can result in improper care or the absence of necessary treatment for individuals experiencing homelessness.

Conclusion

Ultimately, barriers on all levels that hinder the accessibility to healthcare have adverse impacts on the health and well-being of individuals who are experiencing homelessness or are vulnerably housed. Specifically, stigma and discrimination are driving factors in perpetuating mistrust in the healthcare system and healthcare providers, leading to hesitation when deciding to seek care. As well, these negative effects are worsened due to the inflexibility of the healthcare system as many systematic barriers prevent even more individuals from getting the treatment they need. While it is important to identify barriers to accessible healthcare, it is equally as crucial to consider the negative impacts on patient care and the steps that can be taken to overcome these obstacles. Many of these barriers lead to either avoidance of care or improper care for the individual, in which both outcomes will have deleterious effects on long term health. That being said, equitable solutions that address the root causes of present barriers must be determined and implemented.

Chapter 4:

Root causes of barriers

to

accessible healthcare

Sahir Dhalla

To treat the cause rather than the symptoms is a philosophy often applied in many fields, from medical areas where it originated to issues in organizations and systems. But it is very difficult to address these causes when they aren't clearly identified beforehand. Every barrier that homeless individuals face to accessible healthcare has its roots in these major areas: the social determinants of health, which are all factors that are non-medical in nature such as income, nutrition, etc; education, including education inequality and current shortcomings in knowledge for the homeless population as well as their providers; and systemic issues, which includes problems that occur as a result of healthcare policies and attitudes of people towards the homeless population. Exploring and understanding these issues and how they occur is a key step in fixing the issue in the long term.

Social Determinants of Health

Over the past few decades, studies have brought to light a new side to the issue of homelessness that was not as widely recognized before, known as social determinants of health. The social determinants of health are those factors that are usually social or economic in nature, but still have a notable impact on the health and well-being of individuals. These are the factors that play a part in shaping someone's daily life, where they grow, work, and live the majority of their present lives. The World Health Organization (WHO) places immense importance upon these factors, pointing out the major and measurable differences they create both among different countries as well as within countries themselves. As one's socioeconomic status improves, a clear trend emerges where these social determinants are alleviated and become easier to manage. These differences in socioeconomic factors create a significant and clearly visible effect, resulting in a near 20-year difference in average life expectancy across the WHO metric of human development that takes into account all major social determinants of health.

Some of the biggest social determinants of health as shown through research as well as anecdotal evidence are income and income support, nutrition and food security, and housing and environmental concerns in homeless shelters (Campbell et al., 2015). It shouldn't be too difficult to imagine how a shortage in any of these can have a negative impact on one's mental and physical health. It is also these factors that, when put together, create circumstances that make it immensely difficult for the homeless population to receive adequate care in any form, and particularly healthcare.

Income and income support are often referred to as the biggest non-medical determinants of one's health. Dorling et al. (2007) showed that income inequality has a high correlation with higher mortality rates worldwide. While mechanisms of this inequality change from nation to nation, the fact remains throughout that those on the lower end of incomes will suffer worse health conditions. For poor and homeless individuals, their income is often insufficient to supply their basic needs of food, housing, sanitation, and others. Lack of financial resources and security lead to a number of issues that are also often cited as the most common barriers that deter homeless individuals from receiving adequate healthcare, including issues like lack of transportation, inadequate healthcare coverage, or the lack of health benefits (Campbell et al., 2015).

Another key social determinant of health that has a major impact on the homeless population appears in the form of nutrition and food security. Many participants in the Campbell et al. (2015) study mentioned how food insecurity and instability often leads to a worsening health condition as well as general malnutrition. While homeless shelters do work to provide sufficient caloric intake, what is often disregarded is the importance of a nutritionally well-balanced diet. An issue that many individuals also face is the lack of nutritional information available. More often than not, the food provided to these people does not have nutritional information available, so they aren't able to figure out how much of each ingredient they're having and thus can't manage it. Housing and environmental concerns are also cited as some social determinants of health that negatively impact the lives of homeless individuals. Air recycling and conditioning occur regularly in homeless shelters, often with inadequate ventilation and other airflow issues. These have been shown to contribute to easier spread of diseases to people who regularly stay in those rooms (Moffa et al., 2019). One client of a homeless shelter mentioned that "if you were in that [shelter] more than two weeks, you start to cough. It was, it was a wonderful little lung infection that stayed with you until you were at least three to four weeks outside of [the shelter]."

Another major issue was the lack of needle deposit boxes that places needed. Improper disposal of used needles poses the risk of injuries to any staff member that works on cleaning areas where they are thrown away or used (Gold, 2011). Environments as a whole in and around homeless shelters are detrimental to the health and wellbeing of the individuals that use the shelters, contributing further to a problem that is already riddled with so many.

Not only do all these social determinants of health create issues on their own, but they combine to make worse conditions too. Lower income combined with nutritionally imbalanced diets and terrible living environments makes it extremely difficult for individuals to remain healthy, even after they have been treated. This often leads to a life of chronic illnesses and issues that return as soon as they are treated by healthcare, if they can access that healthcare. And then it becomes a continuous cycle of treating the symptoms that continuously show up, putting out fires over and over again without removing the fuel and spark that causes them in the first place. As long as there exists this big of an issue with the social determinants of health, there will be barriers that prevent the homeless from receiving adequate healthcare.
The social determinants of health have a clear and marked impact on the health and wellbeing of any population, but these impacts

are more pronounced on the homeless population. From income to the environment around us, everything changes and impacts both our physical and mental health. A deficiency in any one of these determinants can lead to issues, but poor or homeless individuals often face a deficiency in almost all of them at once. Because of the severity of their conditions with regards to these determinants, combined with the lack of support they currently receive when it comes to improving these conditions, homeless individuals are often condemned to a repeating cycle of issues that perpetrate further issues and inevitably create barriers that make it near-impossible for many to receive the healthcare that they may need. But while the social determinants are impactful, some of them still seem to be symptoms of bigger issues.

Education

One such factor that can be seen as being the root of inequalities in the social determinants of health across the population is education, or the lack thereof. This lack of education refers to a number of things, from the support received during early childhood development to education about governmental benefits and how to access them to sanitation and preventing the spread of contagious diseases. The impact of education even extends into other factors, creating lasting impacts on social determinants like income even decades after these discrepancies and issues may have occurred.

Income and wages are the most impactful social determinants of health, and they are immensely impacted by education. Without adequate income, individuals are unable to supply their basic necessities like food and shelter and are usually unable to get adequate healthcare for any issues that they may face. Trends in the US and Canada over the past 20 years and more clearly show that higher wages are consistently correlated with higher attainment of education, and there is a continuing trend towards increasing differences in wages based on education an individual receives (Hahn and Truman, 2015). Having a higher level of education completed almost always is associated with higher wages or income earned, allowing for individuals to better accommodate all their needs and healthcare necessities.

But it isn't just personal income that dictates one's access to benefits that healthcare provides. It is also heavily impacted by the individual's parents' incomes. When the family has a higher overall income, they are better equipped to provide the child with a stable education, first through early childhood development, then public education systems. They then have the ability to send their kids off the university to complete post-secondary education and receive a degree. Parental income is often a good predictor of the child's income success in the future. While a system like this allows successful parents to ensure the comfort and success of their children, the issue comes in when less fortunate parents, such as homeless families, are unable to break out of this cycle. Because of their lack of income, they are unable to continue a stable education for their child, leading to a perpetuating cycle that keeps generations stuck in the same circumstances.

The National Institutes of Health (NIH) and the WHO both also recognize that basic education is an essential facet of health, and one that is far too often overlooked. Studies by the NIH have shown that a lack of education contributes to overall worse health because the individual lacks basic knowledge, the ability to reason, key social interaction skills, and emotional capacities such as self-awareness and emotional regulation (Hahn and Truman, 2015). Education works to improve cognitive health, which is a major priority as it keeps mental health and the central nervous system in place, much like exercise keeps the physical body healthy. Inequality in education impacts all of these systems of the body and parts of one's entire life for decades after the circumstance happens to the person, and this issue has even been shown to increase with age. Fighting this inequality is one of the main ways to fight the root cause of the issues that homeless individuals face when attempting to access the healthcare that many desperately need.

Besides these long-term impacts that education has on the health and well-being of populations, there are also more immediate issues that must be resolved in existing homeless groups. The first of these is to do with governmental benefits and educating homeless individuals on which they would be eligible for as well as how to take advantage of them if they are ever to improve their living conditions. A study by Campbell et al. (2015) showed that while many of the homeless population in Alberta were eligible for governmental benefits, be it financial or otherwise, a striking number of them were unaware of these benefits or of the processes to go through to acquire them.

There also seems to be a general gap in education about health and wellness, particularly with regards to diseases. Because many of the homeless population are not aware of the symptoms of illnesses and diseases, they are unable to recognize when things are wrong or their situation is unhealthy, and are thus unmotivated to seek help. A participant in the study commented on this lack of education, pointing out that the homeless communities also don't know properly how to reduce the spread of viruses or bacteria that cause diseases. He goes on to highlight efforts that need to be made in effectively conveying the information by "breaking it down to their level."

Education inequality and deficiencies have extremely detrimental impacts on the ability of homeless individuals to get access to healthcare and change their circumstances. From early childhood development, all the way through school and post-secondary education, this inequality has a definite impact on communities across the country. And with such severe impacts that it has, it truly is a shame that it is a facet of the issue that is being so dreadfully overlooked. But besides these major long-term issues, there are also immediate changes that must be made. Education about benefits and avoiding contagious diseases must become a regular part of the resources homeless individuals are provided with and should be seen as just as important, if not as immediate, as things like food and shelter.

Systemic Issues

Systemic discrimination is often used to describe policies, patterns of behaviour, or certain practices that are part of the structure of an organization or system which cause or perpetuate disadvantages against populations of a certain kind, and these issues are rampant in healthcare against homeless individuals. From the priority of types of diseases treated, to the attitude of healthcare staff when it comes to homeless individuals, systemic issues create a host of other problems that prevent homeless individuals from receiving the level of healthcare that they need. Systemic discrimination, along with education and the social determinants of health, is at the root of the barriers to healthcare faced by the homeless population.

Prevention is better than cure is an age-old saying that we are familiar with, but it is not something practiced enough in today's healthcare and homeless support systems. Many individuals who are homeless often face a consistent but quick decline of their health, often facing several chronic issues due to their circumstances that lead to larger acute problems, but most healthcare fails to prioritize chronic issues, reducing the attention homeless individuals may get (Campbell et al., 2015). While focusing on immediate issues such as someone going hungry or not getting enough nutrients is an essential facet of maintaining health, disregarding preventative measures such as up to date immunizations does not do anyone any favours. One of the providers interviewed by Campbell et al. (2015) mentioned that the biggest gap in providing for homeless people is between what it appears that they need compared to what they truly need to benefit them in the long term.

General attitudes towards homeless people, both by healthcare staff and others, have major impacts that act as further barriers against homeless individuals getting help. Several people interviewed in the study mentioned stories where they or someone they knew was treated worse than other patients once they were identified as being homeless.

One provider mentioned that several patients were "hassled by security and they got kicked out right away before they could get assessed," while others noted how judgemental the new staff could be, making people feel unwelcome and increasing the general anxiety surrounding hospital or clinic visits, making them far less inclined to seek out help. The system itself, especially in newer facilities, also seems more hostile towards homeless individuals and it makes them easily identifiable too. Healthcare workers also often disregard the immense impact that homelessness has on one's health, causing them to ignore or downplay the impact of chronic issues that the individual faces. Patients also often feel as though they are cared about less because of some workers who assume that it would be pointless to help a homeless individual or explain their health concerns, especially because they already live in such terrible conditions. If anything, though, it seems common sense that the opposite should be occurring. Seeing the terrible situation that homeless individuals are already in, they should be receiving more attention and more information about their condition and how to alleviate it, rather than ignoring it because of how difficult it would be for the person to remain healthy. And in addition to these efforts, there must also be greater awareness of the basic essentials that homeless individuals lack, such as transport and a steady support system.
One client in the study mentioned how a peer was discharged in the middle of the night from the hospital, leaving them with no means of transportation and essentially forcing them to walk back home.

These studies and anecdotes of the systemic issues in Canada's healthcare system clearly show that this is not an isolated or small incident, but rather a series of issues as a result of an unwilling and unhelpful system. To truly make a change and reduce the barriers facing homeless individuals when they access healthcare, the root of these issues must be addressed. Social determinants of health and their impacts need to be better understood, not just by homeless individuals but those who are in charge of policies for them and those who are in positions to provide healthcare to them. Education inequality must be addressed, helping to smooth out the long-term issues that are caused as a result of these discrepancies. As a whole, the current system prevents individuals from ever breaking out of this cycle.

Chapter 5:

Impact of COVID-19 on the homeless population

Darla Chlœ Daniva

Introduction

Poverty does not only occur in underdeveloped countries but in more developed countries as well. The state of being in poverty is one of the leading causes of homelessness today. With the impact of COVID-19, the number of people who suffer from becoming homeless has increased rapidly. Most importantly, the people who already suffer from homelessness face a more significantly negative impact than the average civilian. The homeless population is mainly caused and formed by unemployment, as people become unable to afford a home where they can seek shelter for their own safety and comfort. Such a marginalised population already faces many issues without a place to call home. The COVID-19 pandemic has also created a rise of fear to the health of the public, and is especially an added risk to the poor as it conflicts with their ability to have access to high quality health care. Fortunately, voluntary and involuntary medical services have been providing medical services to the ones in need, like the homeless. The government, varying on location, aims to aid the homeless with issues such as financial support and healthcare. It is important to note that the sections being discussed refer to different topics with respect to the homeless population varying by location. This chapter will focus on the negative impacts, as well as support, towards the homeless population due to the COVID-19 global pandemic.

Unemployment

With the COVID-19 pandemic and its introduction to the majority of the public, there was a huge shock in terms of unemployment(cite). This shock caused several major and local businesses to shut down, which has resulted in a rise in unemployment(cite). Those working in local businesses and who are self-employed were affected the most(cite). The increase in unemployment leads to poverty, which in turn causes homelessness. This global issue resulted in many civilians not being able to afford necessities like rent or insurance, leading to poverty and homelessness. When the COVID-19 outbreak had begun, it was recorded that approximately 3.3 million people had already filed for unemployment insurance claims by March 21, indicating the first wave of major job loss that had occurred globally (Şahin et al., 2020). As more people become unemployed, uncertainty about estimates of future unemployment rates and homelessness are more often being discussed. An unemployment rate was estimated by the Federal Reserve Bank of Cleveland to be around 16% in May 2021(Şahin et al., 2020). Even though there may be estimated decreases in unemployment, that does not make up for the loss or lowered quality of healthcare and other basic necessities available to the public, to be sufficient.

Even though unemployment is a major factor in poverty and has risen as a factor towards homelessness, it is not the only one. There are of course many other factors which can be taken into consideration that have potentially led people to go homeless, such as natural disasters or robbery. With this taken into factor, there are already many people that have become homeless even before the pandemic. These other factors cause issues that must be discussed, as they have been put into the light more than ever due to COVID-19.

Detriments to Physical and Mental Health

The public must also not forget those who are already suffering from homelessness and facing major conflict with their physical and mental health, compared to the general population. These people now need support more than ever. The consequences of unemployment may cause deteriorating mental health as loss, anxiety, and terror becomes evoked. People already unemployed now have increased difficulty in finding a job, making them more at risk for complications like depression and a lack of nutrients. The homeless population currently lacks the necessary physical and mental quality of health even more due to the costs of the COVID-19 pandemic(cite). More than ever, people need to follow stay-at-home orders and isolate themselves from the dangerous disease that can be deadly to people. Health needs must also be of quality care, which unfortunately tends to be an issue towards the homelessness. Emotionally and physically, every person should have the right to access good health. Many people who have gone homeless usually seek safety in groups or at shelters, where social distancing is not an option. Unfortunately, many of these areas are now having to shut down or limit their capacities due to restrictions. This means that these people have a higher risk of contracting the COVID-19 disease (Parkes et al., 2021). Although there has already been a requested demand to improve healthcare options the homeless currently experience, there is an important issue that must also be addressed. These people already often feel stigmatised and treated badly when they do seek health care, as they feel they may be judged or misdiagnosed due to bias (Howells et al., 2021). With the delivery of services being forced to rapidly transition into online methods, services like healthcare may not be as accessible as before to those who cannot afford technology, as it creates a "digital-divide" (Howells et al., 2021). And even if granted the accessibility to technology, homeless people who have had no experience with such technology may struggle to adapt as there is no current evidence that suggests otherwise (Howells et al., 2021).

A study was conducted in Edinburgh, Scotland to assess the impact of COVID-19 and the city's response across homeless and healthcare centres (Parkes et al., 2021). There have been major changes in the services delivered to the homeless not only limited to healthcare, but also services that include proper housing and social needs. The experiment was conducted by Parkes and colleagues by interviewing individuals who either had experience with homelessness or are currently homeless. The results of this experiment indicated that there is significant evidence, at least in one city center of Scotland, to suggest that the homeless population do face additional challenges from the global pandemic and its impact. For example, the homeless population faced a decrease in services that provide substance use treatment and harm reduction, which are two important these marginalized groups must face today (Parkes et al., 2021). COVID-19 poses amore significant risk to substance and alcohol abusers (Parkes et al., 2021). Furthermore, with pharmacies being closed and alcohol distribution being reduced, the homeless population may also be negatively affected by the symptoms of withdrawal. Withdrawals related to alcohol paired with improper treatment can result in detriments to an individual's health or even death (Parkes et al., 2021). Because of the closure of bars, alcoholic beverage distribution (due to being labelled as non-essential), and government-regulated drug dispensaries, the majority of users move towards the dangerous use of illicit drugs (Parkes et al., 2021). This experiment represents just one of the many occurrences that are happening around the world, which are problematic to the homeless. Sadly, mortality in the homeless population has been known to be 2-5 times higher in its standard mortality population than in its standard-age population (van Rüth et al., 2021). This statistic is unacceptable as every death counts, and with the current restrictions to the homeless population, it has been rapidly increasing worldwide (Parkes et al., 2021). The marginalised population is seen as 'super spreaders' as they are more mobile and without safe and sanitary housing, which may be due to the government's neglect of quality health and safety for them during these tough times (van Rüth et al., 2021). This kind of neglect makes it more of a challenge to face for the homeless as they are perceived to be more at risk to suffer from the severe effects of the disease. By trying to deal with a fluctuating, yet mostly high mortality and existing infectious disease rate, the homeless population requires a greater amount of medical protection and attention from the virus (van Rüth et al., 2021). The basic necessities of physical and mental health should be available and attainable to everyone, which definitely includes the homeless population.

Support For Homeless Population During The COVID-19 Pandemic

As there becomes a rise in people continuing to live through homelessness, there becomes an increased need in support for them. The COVID-19 pandemic has also brought positive action to the light. Thankfully, there has been an increase in teamwork within the community, and more importantly, this means implanting new services to reduce harm (Parkes et al., 2021). The government, community, and generally the generosity of humanity are coming closer together to help each other during the difficulties of living through a global pandemic. As mentioned in the previous section, an experiment had been conducted by Parkes and colleagues to determine the negative impact on the homeless population in order to improve responses to the pandemic worldwide. Many other studies have been conducted or currently are being conducted to be used as something to improve from. Edinburgh has a widely-known program run by The Salvation Army, which is an international charitable program offered by the Christian church (Parkes et al., 2021). The program provides the basic services such as mental and physical healthcare as well as other necessities in an individual's lifestyle such as shower facilities and social activities (Parkes et al., 2021). The Center is not only specifically for dealing with the effects of substance abuse, but also for those who need holistic support (Parkes et al., 2021).

Of course, offering support during the pandemic is not easy. For example, there are huge costs the government must agree to balance and spend (Parkes et al., 2021). By not having enough money to support the homeless during a pandemic, there becomes limited and necessary resources. In the study conducted by Parkes and others, people from the homeless population were put and crowded into a hotel. As a result of rapid housing once it was available, people were rushing and attempting to go over capacities at many hotels or homeless shelters (Parkes et al., 2021). This caused people to become more aggressive and cause violence (Parkes et al., 2021). Some of the reasons these events would occur would be because of fights over not being able to keep shelter at organizations, which would risk the safety of not only other homeless people staying at these centers, but to the staff as well. Also, many homeless patients were not too fond of abiding to COVID-19 laws or respecting the current encouraged restrictions (Parkes et al., 2021). However, the safety and health of every human and animal being must be protected and considered a priority. This means basic but high quality mental and physical healthcare should be accessible by everyone around. Unfortunately, there are many areas where the world can improve on when it comes to this.

Conclusion

With the COVID-19 pandemic came many advantages and disadvantages on the impact for the homeless population. People worldwide were adding to the number of the marginalised population as many businesses file for bankruptcy or end up closing. While people lost jobs they had also begun to lose their ability to afford the comfort of their home and other basic necessities. The homeless population that had already been suffering from poverty in comparison to the general population now suffered more than ever during the global pandemic. People are thankfully coming together to help one another survive this pandemic, however it is now always easy. Despite the pros and cons of the impact on the homeless population, there is hope it will only be temporary and that more services will be opened to them at this time. People hope that the system will improve even more from before the pandemic began, as they crave and demand positive change.

Chapter 6:

Effect of homelessness

on

hunger and nutrition

Margarita Liubetskaya

Introduction

As a whole, nutrition has been a hot topic throughout various sources of media over the recent years. From "fad diets' ' to "mukbangs' ', both extremes of the eating and nutritional spectra have been widely popular and at the same time largely subjected to controversy. The underlying problem stems from the average person not being educated on or implementing proper nutrition into their diet. Another large portion of the population that is aware of the nutritional guidelines, often chooses to not abide by them or is simply not able to. This chapter will explore these two opposing issues by examining nutrition as a whole, the over and undereating general populations, exploring where the homeless population fits on the continuum, determining where it all goes wrong, and learning the implications of improper nutrition specifically within the homeless community and vice versa; the implications of homelessness on hunger and nutrition.

A Brief Background on Nutrition

Canada's Food Guide

Before discussing homelessness and hunger, it is only fitting that we establish a baseline. So, what constitutes "good" nutrition and how do we achieve it? According to Canada's most recent 2019 food guide, an individual striving to optimize his or her health should eat a variety of healthy foods each day. This includes roughly half the serving portion consisting of a variety of fruits and vegetables which have important nutrients like fibre, vitamins, and minerals. A quarter of the intake serving should consist of proteins, including plant-based proteins. Which again increases intake of important nutrients: protein, vitamins, and minerals. Lastly, another quarter of the daily intake should consist of whole grain foods which are a healthier alternative to refined grains and, once again, include important nutrients. Additionally, the new food guide emphasizes making water the drink of choice which helps reduce extra intake of calories, sodium, sugar, and saturated fat ("Canada's Food Guide", 2021).

Differences Between The New And Old Food Guide

The new food guide aims to minimize disease risk and is developed on the basis of not being complex or confusing/difficult to use. It was designed based on scientific information that considers the diversity in Canadian culture, the environment and the impact that the human diet has on it, and social determinants of health. These were not a priority of the old, 2007, food guide. Additionally, the new guide puts emphasis on variety rather than portions and supporting healthy eating patterns that last. The information is not influenced by beef or dairy farmers, eliminating the bias seen in the 2009 version.

Physical and Mental Health Benefits of Proper Nutrition

Though this portion might seem more intuitive, the benefits of a proper balanced diet should still be mentioned in this chapter. Starting with a balanced diet, the nutrients it provides have significant health benefits. Fruit and vegetables supply dietary fibre, as mentioned earlier, which is directly linked to lowering risk of cardiovascular disease, diabetes, and obesity (Slavin & Lloyd, 2012). The fiber in whole grains also reduces how much cholesterol we take into our bloodstream, and helps to increase fecal bulk, which helps prevent constipation and other gastrointestinal disorders. Another source states that reducing saturated fat intake, like the kind present in dairy products, also leads to a reduction in cardiovascular mortality and strokes (Westhoek et al., 2014). These are just the physical benefits.

In terms of mental wellbeing, there are studies present that actually deduce that students who have a higher number of vegetable servings per day reportedly scored higher "happiness scores", ultimately proving that there is a correlation between nutrition and mental health (Lesani et al., 2016). Additionally, vegans, who arguably are an extreme example, have a higher intake of vegetables and fruits, as well as a limited dairy intake, and report having less stress and anxiety in their day to day lives (Beezhold et al., 2014). With this being said, it seems natural that many would be inclined to incorporate the balanced diet recommended by the food guide, but is this what really happens?

General Population Statistics

General Population Awareness

Overall, when discussing the nutrition of the general population, we can analyze how many people, in this case Canadians, are meeting the required criteria to be considered as having a balanced diet according to the food guide. Research by Statistics Canada was conducted reporting that Canadians are "very aware" of Canada's Food Guide, with 80% of interviewees having heard of it. Yet, of the people who had heard of the guide, 84% of women had actually looked through one, compared to only 66% of men. The major reason reported for not looking through the food guide was a lack of interest, with an overwhelming 79% of respondents giving this reason. Looking at the "unaware" side of things, 53% of the participants stated their source of healthy eating information was "none", followed by "general research," at 24%, and a miserable 8.7% reported actually using the food guide (Slater & Mudryj, 2018). Essentially, this means that while most people are aware that a recommended balanced diet exists, a significant portion chooses to not abide by it or attempt to inform themselves on it.

The Two Extremes

As unfortunate as it is, simply put - the average Canadian is not eating a diet that promotes optimal health. This can be seen when taking a closer look at those categories of people who, due to various reasons, choose to not follow, learn, or even those who are simply unaware of the need for a balanced diet. We can split these people into two categories: people who overeat and people who undereat the necessary amount of nutrients. From the overeating perspective, in 2018, 26.8% of Canadians were classified as obese, and 36.3% were labelled overweight. This means that 63.1% of the population, that year, had increased health risks and were linked to many chronic diseases including hypertension, type

2 diabetes, cardiovascular disease, osteoarthritis, and certain cancers (Statistics Canada, 2019). According to the World Health Organization, these major diet-related diseases are caused in large part due to unhealthy diets and lifestyles such as consuming too many calories, too few fruits and vegetables, and too much salt. The lack of a proper, variety-filled, nutritious, diet is a crisis and has in some essence reached epidemic status as it continues to rise and affect more and more people every day (WHO, 2015).

Conversely, and in no way any less critical, undereating presents significant threats to human health despite being less prominent or commonly discussed. The reason for it being the lesser emphasized extreme, in the context of Canada or, more broadly, North America, is that malnutrition is commonly and falsely associated with the myth that it is only prevalent in developing nations. This, however, is a huge misconception. An estimated 45% of hospitalized medical and surgical patients in Canada are reported to be malnourished due to prolonged hospitalization that results in muscle mass loss (Holmes, 2018). Outside of the hospital environment, there are more factors contributing to undereating, such as food insecurity. Food insecurity is defined as the disruption of food intake or eating patterns because of lack of money and other resources, and between the years of 2011 and 2012, 8.4% of Canadians, 1 098 900 people, fell under this category ("Household food insecurity in Canada statistics and graphics
(2011 to 2012) - Canada.ca", 2020).

Furthermore, almost half of Canadians aged 18-to-34 (47%) and aged 35-to-54 (46%) went on a diet over the past twelve months in an attempt to lose weight, proving that situational and financial factors aside, there is a strong social norm component to nutrition. This is reinforced since many Canadians achieved their dietary goal not necessarily by implementing the suggested guidelines but instead, listening to statements frequently discussed within the subject of nutrition, regardless of accuracy. Carbs are bad, antibiotics in food-producing animals can lead to antibiotic resistance in humans, genetically modified foods are unhealthy for you, and organic foods are way healthier than non-organic foods, are examples of some of these claims ("Two-in-Five Canadians Tried to Lose Weight Over the Past Year", 2021).

Where Homelessness Fits In

Overwhelming statistics aside, what does all of this mean and how does it relate to homelessness?

As mentioned in chapter one of this book, around 235,000 Canadians are currently experiencing homelessness. Expanding more on the term "food insecurity" which we also mentioned earlier, an approximate 90% of study participants reflecting the homeless community, admitted to experiencing food insecurity. Of that, 67% of participants experienced severe food insecurity and 22.5% fell under the moderate category. It should be noted that qualitative data suggests that all participants were food insecure based on their food acquisition practices, food accessibility, and diet quality (D'andreamatteo & Slater, 2018). This is represented by the average meal intake of a homeless male or female not meeting any of the recommendations set out by Canada's food guide and a majority of energy coming from "other foods" instead of the required food groups. The mean intakes from all the food groups were considered extremely low. Most individuals failed to consume any whole grains or dark green/orange vegetables. It is no surprise that most fail to meet their nutritional needs (Li et al., 2009).

Taking a step away from Canada and looking at the U.S., their data also revealed that the homeless population was insufficient in vegetables, fruit, dairy, and protein. What is interesting is that of the 313 participants in a smaller scale study, 29.4% were overweight and 39% were obese, this was an unexpected result for obvious reasons (Martins et al., 2015). Despite this being a smaller study, many other results confirm this. One particular study showed that the majority (57%) of chronically homeless adults were overweight or obese and chronically homeless adults who were female, or Hispanic, appeared to be at particular risk for obesity (Tsai & Rosenheck, 2013). From this, it can be deduced that similarly to malnutrition not being an issue in developed countries, homelessness and lack of obesity is another misconception. In reality these two things may very well coincide and thrive off each other.

In fact, a study published by Urban Health concluded that only 1.6% of homeless adults were underweight. It states that, "Although underweight has been traditionally associated with homelessness, this study suggests that obesity may be the new malnutrition of the homeless in the United States." (Koh et al., 2012). When examining the homeless vs non-homeless populations used in this study, looking specifically at patterns within sexes and age groups, obesity is in some cases more prevalent in the non-homeless population. This suggests that perhaps as a whole, the view on malnutrition and nutrition itself needs to change to adapt to these new numbers, as well as prove that homelessness is indeed, a barrier for proper nutrition. The big question when seeing this is evidently – why does this occur? What makes obesity so prevalent in the homeless community?

Ultimately, insufficiency in nutrients like vitamin A, zinc, magnesium, potassium and selenium, as well as increased consumption in saturated fat and dairy is not surprising when considering the fee discrepancies associated with a balanced diet. When comparing the price of a diet rich in fruits, vegetables, fish, and nuts with one comprised largely of processed foods, meat, and refined carbohydrates, there is an approximate $2,200 difference per year in a family of four ("Poor diet | Food Policy for Canada", n.d.). Additionally, another study reports that consuming a U.S. MyPlate diet consisting of only fresh fruits and vegetables is the most expensive diet (Mulik & Haynes-Maslow, 2017), and coincidently, many nutritionists say fast food is one of the worst things in the American diet. Its calories, trans fats, lack of fiber and added sugars and processed carbohydrates diminish all value. In fact, "If you're looking at the Dollar Menu in terms of how much food you get it really appears as a good bargain," said Connie Schneider, a nutrition adviser for Fresno County in California, "But if you're looking at it as how many nutrients are you getting for a dollar, it's the least economical." ("Salads or No, Cheap Burgers Revive McDonald's", 2021). Essentially, what ends up happening is people who are in a financially tough situation are unable to afford better nutrition, they settle for quantity over quality, and this is detrimental in the long run. In the case where a homeless individual chooses to not go down the fast-food route but is still unable to afford a more nutritious diet, malnutrition occurs, creating a lose-lose situation.

Conclusion

In conclusion, nutrition is a complicated subject for many. It can be confusing to decipher through the common misconceptions and false claims that are so prominent and common in today's media. Another challenge is escaping the social pressure and norms that also shape how we perceive the food we eat. Even when data is presented to maximise simplicity and help guide people, it does not necessarily mean the resource will be utilized. In fact, in the case of the Canadian food guide, the general public in most cases ignored the recommendations which means that there are two main categories of people – the uninformed and the uninterested. When considering nutrition and homelessness, another consideration must be at play, and that is affordability. Whether the homeless population is able to access information on nutrition or if they care enough to, really has little to do with the reality that they simply cannot afford a more balanced diet. This leads to two possible outcomes, being malnourished or obese, the ladder being the unexpected and yet more common outcome.

Chapter 7:

Effect of homelessness on infectious diseases

Mohathir Sheikh

Homelessness is a common problem in North America. HUD's Annual Point-in-Time Count found that seventeen out of every 10 000 people in the United States were facing homelessness on a single night in January of 2019 (State of Homelessness, 2020). In the United States, it is estimated about 3.5 million adults and children experience homelessness every year (Leung et al., 2008). In Canada, tens of thousands of people are homeless. Cities such as Toronto, Ontario can have around 5000 individuals that are homeless on any given night. Homelessness is associated with numerous behavioral, social environmental risks including poor living conditions and limited access to healthcare organizations which increases the risk of homeless individuals contracting many communicable infections (Badiaga et al., 2008). Furthermore, the facilities such as drop-in centres and soup kitchens which provide services to the homeless population face increased risk of outbreaks (Leung et al., 2008). The outbreak of infectious diseases from the homeless population can become a serious public health concern and as a result many consider homelessness a growing social and public health problem in the world (Badiaga et al., 2008; Leung et al., 2008).

Infectious Disease Rates in Homeless Populations

Epidemiologic studies of homeless populations have reported the following prevalence rates for infectious diseases (Badiaga et al., 2008):

- HIV infections rates between 6.2% - 35%
- Hepatitis B virus (HBV) infection rates between 17% - 30%
- Hepatitis C virus (HCV) infection rates between 12% - 30%
- Active tuberculosis (TB) between 1.2% - 6.8%
- Scabies between 3.8% - 56%
- Body louse infestations between 7% - 22%
- Bartonella quintana infection between 2% - 30%

One study found that Hepatitis C rates among the homeless population in Toronto are 29 times higher than the rest of the Canadian population (Aleman, 2016). The studies have found that the prevalence rates for these transmissible diseases vary greatly based on living conditions. A study conducted in the United States found that homeless persons have HIV infection rates up to 16 times higher than those living in stable homes (Aleman, 2016). The United Nations describes "absolute homelessness" as persons without any physical shelter. They also describe "relative homelessness" as persons who have a physical shelter; however, the shelter does not meet the basic standards of health and safety such as access to water, sanitation, personal safety, and protection from the elements. Homeless persons that fall under the "relative homelessness" definition generally sleep in vehicles, abandoned buildings and other areas not intended for human habitation. These persons also tend to be frequent injection drug users and will often engage in risky sexual behaviours. Both behaviours expose them to blood borne and sexually transmitted diseases such as HIV, HCV, and HBV. Homeless persons sleeping in shelters are exposed to different health risks. Overcrowding with lack of proper ventilation in the shelters increases the spread of airborne diseases such as TB. Additionally, the lack of personal hygiene and clean clothing increases the risk of developing scabies, exposure to body lice and contracting louse-borne diseases. The homeless population that are able to find proper shelter, whether it is with family, friends, or hotel rooms still face health risks similar to those living in absolute and relative homelessness. In general, these homeless persons are also frequent injection drug users and are characterised as engaging in risky sexual activities which would expose them to the same blood-borne and sexually transmitted diseases prevalent within the rest of the homeless population.

Infectious Disease Treatment in Homeless Population

Treatments for infectious diseases in the homeless population are complicated due to barriers homeless persons face when trying to access healthcare services (Aleman, 2016). These barriers can be lack of funds for medication, not having an ID or a health card, lack of transportation to healthcare facilities, feelings of stigmatization at health visits, and may not easily be able to follow treatment schedules. Unfortunately, the existing barrier means many homeless persons are unable to get proper treatment from the health care system and must rely on using emergency services when the disease gets too burdensome. For homeless persons that are able to access and receive treatment, they are generally still living in unhealthy environments which will increase their risk of contracting other infectious diseases.

HIV

In the case of homeless persons living with HIV, there are additional insights that can be drawn from their difficult circumstances. In general, homeless persons have a higher level of HIV present in the blood compared to non homeless persons living with HIV. Increased levels of HIV viral load will result in advanced presentation of the HIV disease and will increase the likelihood of transmitting the disease to others if the individual engages in risky drug injection or sexual behaviours (Leung et al., 2008). Through the use of effective antiretroviral medications and access to regular medical care, the HIV viral load can be reduced. Unfortunately for homeless persons living with HIV, they are more likely to delay receiving HIV care, more likely to have poorer access to regular HIV care, less likely to receive optimal antiretroviral therapy and less likely to adhere to therapy and treatment plans. This is generally due to a combination of reasons. In addition to the barriers the homeless population faces when trying to access health care mentioned earlier, the homeless patients may receive less than optimal care due to the choices made by their physician. Some physicians may withhold antiretroviral treatment or prescribe suboptimal treatments due to reservations they may have regarding the homeless individual's ability to properly adhere to the dosing schedule and show up for the follow up appointments.

Interventions for the Homeless Population

HIV and Hepatitis

As mentioned previously, those engaging in risky sexual behaviours, such as unsafe sex, having multiple sexual partners, or involved in sex work are at an increased risk of contracting HIV (Leung et al., 2008; Wolitski et al., 2007). Frequent injection drug users who share needles, syringes and other equipment are also at high risk of getting infected with HIV. In order to control the spread of HIV in the homeless population, intensive intervention programs need to be implemented. Studies have shown that a lack of housing operates as an environmental influence that interacts with other risk factors such as substance use, risky sexual and injection practices, sexual abuse, physical violence, poor mental health, and sex work (Wolitski et al., 2007). Data has also shown that homeless persons are less likely to reduce their HIV risks compared to individuals living in a stable housing environment. However, this does not mean a homeless person can not change their behaviour to reduce their HIV risk. In fact, studies have shown that behavioral interventions have been successful in significantly reducing risk behaviour in this subpopulation (Leung et al., 2008; Wolitski et al., 2007). An intensive intervention program targeting homeless youth achieved a significant reduction in unprotected sex acts over 12 months and drug use over 12 months (Badiaga et al., 2008). The program involved grouping shelter staff and residents into small groups to provide training and access to health care systems. The program also made condoms easily available and at no cost. This program, along with others, provided proof on the feasibility of helping reduce the prevalence of HIV and hepatitis in homeless populations, using intensive intervention programs. Other programs focused on drug treatment such as supervised injection sites have been successful in not only reducing the number of HIV infections but also reducing the number of overdoses (Ng et al., 2017).

In terms of reducing HBV infections, some studies have shown the plausibility of using syringe exchange sites to administer HBV vaccinations (Badiaga et al., 2008). By offering the HBV vaccinations at the syringe exchange locations, the vaccination program was able to offer more opportunities to frequent injection drug users to get vaccinated. A study in New Haven, Connecticut successfully administered two doses of the HBV vaccination to 77% of the sample population and fully vaccinated 66% of the sample population by administering all three doses of the vaccine.

Tuberculosis and Airborne Diseases

The spread of TB among the homeless is quick and often results in infecting over 50% of the residents in the shelter (Badiaga et al., 2008). To control the spread of TB, the individual cases must be caught early before having a chance to spread. Contact tracing all the people an infected person had close contact with, and effective TB treatments can help reduce the spread of the disease. Many shelters in the United States now have mandatory shelter based screening, which has led to a reduction of TB transmission among the homeless

Ways to Control the Prevalence of Infectious Disease

During the SARs outbreak, there were changes made at many shelters and drop in centres to help control the spread of infection (Leung et al., 2008). Having staff use gloves and masks, increased surface cleaning and disinfection, and encouraging frequent handwashing or hand sanitizer use were all part of the enhanced basic infection control procedures implemented by these locations. However, there were many challenges that arose as well. The lack of specific guidelines and supply constraints meant there was a large variability in the policies being implemented across agencies. Many homeless agencies are not classified as health care facilities; therefore, health officials did not arrange for personal protective equipment to be supplied to these locations. Supplies were sent to city operations but the independent community based shelters were left to purchase supplies on their own. An unexpected problem also appeared after alcohol based hand sanitizer was placed in the shelters. Some residents would drink the entire bottle of sanitizer solution due to its alcohol content.

Many lessons were learned from the SARs outbreak and now there are new infection-control plans in place that considers the special needs of the homeless population. Health officials and representatives from public health, shelter services, and community agencies were established to prepare an outbreak response planning guide for homeless service providers. In the event a future outbreak occurs, shelter providers are trained in using illness-surveillance records to track symptom clusters among shelter residents. The National Institute for Health and Clinical Excellence recommends the following guidelines to better treat, control, and decrease the cases of TB, hepatitis C, and HIV among the homeless population (Aleman, 2016):

- Simultaneous screenings for TB, hepatitis C, and HIV
- Transportation and housing support as well as ensuring adequate nutrition
- Active case-finding screenings (should not be restricted to symptomatic patients)
- Needle exchange programmes
- Free condom distributions
- Community health centres in large cities
- Better access to health care

The Tuberculosis Prevention and Control in Canada: A Federal Framework for Action was also announced in 2014, by the Government of Canada. This framework for action addresses the underlying risk factors related to the social determinants of health in preventing and controlling the spread of TB.

Although these are important recommendations, the inequalities, and barriers the homeless face when trying to access health care needs to be addressed first. Without changes in the current system, the homeless population will continue to be a high-risk group to contract communicable diseases with the potential to become a public health concern should an infectious outbreak occur.

Conclusion

High prevalence rates of infectious diseases in the homeless population continues to be a growing global problem. Many studies have linked the high disease prevalence rates with unstable housing conditions. Furthermore, the existence of barriers to accessing health care for the homeless population, in addition to their existing behavioural, social, and environmental risks, play a large role in preventing the homeless population from receiving help and treatment when they need it. Despite changes and improvements being made to help reduce and prevent infectious disease outbreaks in the homeless population, there still needs to be more work done in establishing better harm reduction programs and support programs. Only then, will we start to see significant improvements in our ability to manage, treat and prevent infectious disease outbreaks.

Chapter 8:

Effect of Homelessness

on

Sexual and Reproductive Health

Sidra Bharmal

Sexual and reproductive health (SRH) is a state of sufficient physical, mental, and social well-being regarding any element of the reproductive system (United Nations Populations Fund, n.d.). Thus, SRH is a human right, yet there are some demographics that struggle with accessing and utilizing quality care and related resources (United Nations Human Rights, n.d.). Homeless persons, particularly those with female reproductive organs, are mentally and physically at risk due to a lack of sexual and reproductive care (SRC), menstrual products, and contraceptives (The Homeless Hub, n.d.).

Inaccessibility and Barriers to SRCs

Unmet health care needs, specifically for SRH, is a common issue among the homeless population. However, this demographic, particularly people with ovaries (PWO), report a higher volume of reproductive health-related cases, including unplanned pregnancies and miscarriages (Cronley et al., 2017). Pregnant PWO who experience homelesessness have a reduced likelihood to receive preconception or prenatal care in their first trimester, and have fewer overall prenatal visits (Azarmehr et al., 2018). Logistical, psychological, educational, and emotional obstacles are the fundamental causes of the minimal usage of these services (Azarmehr et al., 2018). In one study, several Canadian women in homeless shelters reported this lack of access to practical and mental support for pregnancy, while additionally feeling judged for their circumstance - and the "lifestyle" that caused it - by the shelter staff (Duchesne, 2015).

Not only are there insufficient prenatal services for the homeless, but there is a limited availability of contraceptives. One 2012 study conducted a survey of the 20 member organizations providing healthcare to the homeless - specifically from the national Health Care for the Homeless Practice-Based Research Network - to investigate the quality and accessibility of the services provided (Saver et al., 2012). Of those, 17 directly provided contraceptive services, 2 referred other locations, and 1 provided none (Saver et al., 2012). Furthermore, all mentioned 17 administered condoms, 15 provided oral contraceptives, 14 had injectable contraceptives, 6 were equipped with intrauterine devices (IUDs), and 2 could provide contraceptive implants (Saver et al., 2012). Therefore, the two most competent and long-term methods of reversible contraception (implants and IUDs) are the least available to the homeless who are in desperate need of them (Saver et al., 2012). Some barriers that should be overcome to improve this situation include additional provider training, increased resources for placement, reduced costs, and further research into potential complications (Saver et al., 2012).

Personal backgrounds play crucial roles in the decisions of individuals affected by homelessness when seeking care. There is a notable percentage of homeless women who experience sexual violence, which generates more incidences of unintended pregnancies and STIs in this population (Wenzel et al., 2001). Homeless youth, a generally more fertile demographic, are especially susceptible to sexual abuse, with 21 to 42% reporting sexual assault, compared to the 1 to 3% of the general youth population (National Sexual Violence Resource Center, n.d.). It would be expected that situations of molestation produce some motivation for homeless people to seek gynecological care, just as it does for their non-homeless counterparts (Wenzel et al., 2001). Instead, there is a reduced probability of homeless victims subsequently visiting a health professional (Wenzel et al., 2001). This is supplemented by the histories of many homeless people as adult survivors of child sexual abuse who are thus psychologically influenced, with negative, trauma-like responses being triggered by gynecological examinations (Wenzel et al., 2001). Homeless rape victims are therefore one of the least likely groups to accept reproductive care, despite being critically in need of receiving these services (Wenzel et al., 2001).

Menstruation

Among adversities that emerge from homelessness, the need for menstrual management is consistently ignored. All individuals who menstruate deserve to do so with dignity, comfort, and safety (Sommer et al., 2020). However, limited accessibility to menstrual products, menstrual stigma, inability to satisfy personal hygiene, and gynecological complications are factors that manufacture the negative menstrual experiences PWO have endured (Sommer et al., 2020).

Little Access to Menstrual Products

It is imperative for homeless persons to have access to feminine hygiene products for sanitation and convenience, just as it is for all other communities. Instead, there is a lack of accessibility, and consequently, homeless persons must invent alternative and riskier methods of menstrual management. Some can only use toilet paper and repeatedly wrap it around their underwear as a makeshift pad (Parrillo & Feller, 2017). Others are further destitute, and must reuse and ruin pieces of cloth, or they are forced to free-bleed (Parrillo & Feller, 2017).

One previous obstacle in purchasing menstrual products was the tampon tax - an additional sales tax applied to these allegedly nonessential products (Weiss-Wolf et al., 2020). It had been decided that feminine hygiene materials were not "treatment or prevention of illness or disease in human beings", despite menses being a common and repeating biological occurrence with risks involved in the neglect of sanitary materials (Parrillo & Feller, 2017). It was therefore a step forward when Canada had this tax abolished, yet the continued commodification of menstrual equipment still poses a barrier to those who struggle with paying for basic necessities (Vora, 2020). People experiencing homeless may then have to decide between these aforementioned self-created menstrual management materials or costly, store-bought items (The Homeless Hub).

Menstrual Stigma

Although menstruation is globally common among the majority of women, it is usually a stigmatized event (Johnston-Robledo & Chrisler, 2020). Often, it is encouraged to keep these occurrences concealed, with menstrual blood itself being treated as an abomination (Johnston-Robledo & Chrisler, 2020). The pervasive hostility towards period blood promotes incredible apprehension of menses stains, being sources of humiliation for many PWO (Johnston-Robledo & Chrisler, 2020). As a homeless person, without money and mobility, it is challenging to conceal menstruation and remain clean (Vora, 2020). Having to accordingly worry about odor and disheveled appearance, along with this general stigmatization of menstrual cycles, can cause homeless persons to feel embarrassed while on their periods with a further potential impact on mental health (Vora, 2020).

Maintenance of Hygiene

Without being equipped to control menstrual bleeding, some menstruating individuals are forced to free-bleed or continue to use the same, soiled products. Clothes then become sullied, contributing to poor overall hygiene (Parrillo & Feller, 2017). Furthermore, insufficient access to other necessities like soap or safer water means that these stained materials cannot be cleansed, or dirty water is relied on to clear up blood. Either way, this homeless population is more vulnerable to infections and poor gynecological health (Parrillo & Feller, 2017).

Gynecological Complications

The frequent use of contaminated materials lead to unclean genitalia which fosters a conducive environment for infections to grow (Parrillo & Feller, 2017). PWO who experience homelessness are therefore more often seen in health clinics for gynecological challenges than other individuals (Sommer et al., 2020). A 2001 study examining this matter found that from their sample of 974 women, the majority had at least one gynecological symptom or condition within the prior 12-month period (Wenzel et al., 2001). Examples include abnormal discharge, burning urination, abnormal period duration, or pelvic pain (Wenzel et al., 2001). More recent and prevailing diagnoses among the PWO population have since been reported to be urinary tract infections (UTIs), yeast infections, and vulvar contact dermatitis (Sommer et al., 2020). Overall, the vulnerability of this demographic to gynecological complications is a significant concern that can be reduced by increased accessibility to menstrual products to improve cleanliness and safety. The supplementary dilemma is that without earlier medical attention for these gynecological problems, unnecessary complications can emerge and be further detrimental to the physical health of homeless PWO (Wenzel et al., 2001).

Birth Control and Pregnancy

Low compared to high income earners are twice more likely not to use contraceptives (Rak, 2018). Meanwhile, homeless youth are further distressed financially, and are more inclined to behave impulsively - with this increased tendency involving risky sexual behaviour (Rak, 2018). Altogether, monetary difficulties limiting the purchase of contraceptives, increased likelihood of sexual activity, and the inaccessibility to preventative and family planning services, contribute to the high susceptibility of STI exposure and unplanned pregnancy in homeless individuals (Rak, 2018).

Approximately 45% of the United States population have experienced an unintended pregnancy (Corey et al., 2020). To contrast, for homeless women, there are nearly 75% of these events (Corey et al., 2020). Furthermore, there is a greater percentage of this population - roughly 94% - that desired to avoid pregnancy (Corey et al., 2020). A valuable preventative factor is the use of birth control, however PWO experiencing homelessness are among the least likely to have access to effective contraceptives (Corey et al., 2020). As a result, approximately 13% of the demographic are pregnant at any given time, being double the rate among the general American population (Corey et al., 2020).

Furthermore, considering the poor reproductive health induced by homelessness, there are several adverse results of pregnancy (Paisi et al., 2020).

Fetal complications in homeless PWO are often also a consequence of inaccessibility of health and prenatal care (Keohane, 2017). For an already vulnerable and marginalized community, the emotional and psychological impact of pregnancy, compounded by the difficulty of childbirth and motherhood, with the additional risk of a negative outcome throughout pregnancy, can have a detrimental effect on these people's lives (Keohane, 2017). The severe possibilities of pregnancy only illuminate the continued and crucial need for accessible birth control in the homeless community.

All PWO should be able to access any contraceptive with the purpose of avoiding pregnancy or STIs, and be provided with enough information to make informed decisions about the type of birth control they want to utilize. Homeless PWO, however, are often lacking quality contraceptive counselling, and effective methods of prevention are regularly unobtainable to them (Corey et al., 2020). Long-acting reversible contraceptives (LARC) are a functional form of birth control that is generally not discussed in contraception counselling, with especially little information being provided to individuals experiencing homelessness (Corey et al., 2020). Without full education, homeless people are likely to make judgments regarding their SRH that are poorer than non-homeless individuals.

There are several other common obstacles with reference to the use of contraceptives, including fear of side effects, cost, and storage (Corey et al., 2020). The particular root of this problem is that despite having universal health care, Canada still does not have wide-spread access to birth control for PWO (The University of British Columbia, 2019). Therefore, not only are homeless persons not provided with sufficient information pertaining to contraceptives, but they are not able to afford accessing the complete range of those products available in Canada (The University of British Columbia, 2019). Nonetheless, the purchase of contraceptives would be irrelevant without a safe environment to store them, or general feelings of easiness around their use (Gelberg et al., 2002).

LGBTQIA2S+

The LGBTQIA2S+ community is disproportionately affected by homelessness. In Canada, between 25 to 40 % of homeless youth identify as a member of this demographic (Casey, 2019). Without financial burden, there is already a large disparity of HIV cases between this community and non-LGBTQIA2S+. Gay, bisexual, and other men who have sex with men (gbMSM) represent 3 to 5 % of the adult male population in Canada, yet they comprised of 48 percent of new HIV cases in 2016 (Casey, 2019). Considering the additional risk of HIV due to monetary burden, LGBTQIA2S+ experiencing homelessness are the most vulnerable to this disease (Rak, 2018).

Generally, there is a lack of proficient SRC for members of the LGBTQIA2S+ community despite the significant influence of autonomy and sexuality on SRH (The Homeless Hub, n.d.). This exists especially for members of the transgender community. One in five individuals from this population have experienced homelessness sometime in their lifetimes (NCTE). This could be due to discrimination when searching for a home, eviction based on their identity, family rejection, violence, or several other reasons rooted in transphobia (NCTE). This community is then further subjected to inequality when facing homelessness through the inadequacy of their reproductive healthcare (The Homeless Hub, n.d.). Gender-based discrimination can cause a struggle to to access competent care, with some instances of refusal of treatment, and a scarcity in LBTQIA2S+ tailored programs (The Homeless Hub, n.d.). Furthermore, transgender individuals who were first assigned female at birth tend to struggle with gender dysphoria, which can influence their preference in menstrual products (The Homeless Hub, n.d.). However, the financial strain that characterizes homelessness limits the freedom of choice, negatively impacting the mental and physical health of this demographic (The Homeless Hub, n.d.). Altogether, this especially emphasizes the necessity of widespread availability of sanitary products for those who cannot afford them (The Homeless Hub, n.d.).

Conclusion

To many, SRH is not a primary concern in their lives. With transportation, financial stability, and cleanliness, SRC is easily accessible for higher income earners (Azarmehr et al., 2018). However, the homeless population is lacking in these qualities, rendering it especially challenging to maintain their SRH. Discomfort is another contributing factor to the infrequency of SRC visits, with both experiences of prejudice from the workers and history of sexual violence causing aversion to those services. Furthermore, the expensive costs of menstrual products that exist despite them being a necessity for menstruating individuals force PWO experiencing homelessness to rely on less safe, self-made materials, or free-bleeding. Both have negative hygienic influences on these people, leading to further mental and physical distress. Likewise, a full range of birth control, and related education are not accessible to this demographic. Therefore, there are increased incidences of STIs and unintended pregnancies, both worsening the emotional and physical state of homeless PWO. The LGBTQIAS2S+ community is especially impacted by this lack of contraceptives, with STIs being especially prevalent among them. Finally, the distinct discrimination and ignorance in SRC systems towards this population, particularly the transgender community, means many of their basic needs are not met. The little availability of menstrual products has a further detrimental effect on persons suffering from gender dysphoria, meaning not only are homeless and transgender nations subject to poorer genitourinary conditions, but their mental health states are likely to suffer as well.

It is fundamental for the overall health of the homeless population for there to be more attention delegated to their special needs in SRH care (Committee on Health Care for Homeless People, 1988). Tailored services should then be developed, with added awareness to the existing diversity in the community (Committee on Health Care for Homeless People, 1988). In the end, everyone deserves to feel safe and supported, and improving accessibility to sexual and reproductive health systems for the homeless is a great step towards that civil right being realized.

Chapter 9:

Effect of homelessness on chronic illnesses/diseases and mortality

Mariyam Sardar

Introduction

According to the World Health Organization, chronic diseases are the leading cause of mortality globally (Merdosy et al., 2020). A study reported that 51.6% of Canadians have at least one chronic disease, and 14.8% of people have more than one (Merdosy et al., 2020). People with low socioeconomic status have a higher rate of chronic diseases due to a lack of nutritious food, safe shelter, secure jobs, and healthcare access (Merdosy et al., 2020). The homeless community is one of the low socioeconomic communities. 85% of homeless people are reported to be diagnosed with at least one chronic disease (Merdosy et al., 2020). Similarly, a study by St. Michael's Hospital in 2011 revealed that 85% of homeless people have at least one chronic health condition, and greater than 50% of the homeless people have a mental illness (South Riverdale Community Health Centre, 2019). Another study has estimated that 235000 Canadians experience homelessness every year (Gilmer & Buccieri, 2020). The 2001 Census of Canada indicated that 14000 individuals were homeless (Nikoo et al., 2015). However, this number is said to be underestimated (Nikoo et al., 2015). In recent years, people experiencing homelessness have increased. A 2013 poll conducted has indicated that 1.3 million Canadians have been homeless at some point in their life in the last five years (Nikoo et al., 2015). In 2007, between 17500 and 35500 people were inadequately sheltered in British Columbia (Nikoo et al., 2015). This chapter will elaborate on the types of illnesses prevalent in the homeless population and the mortality rates of chronic diseases among the homeless.

Chronic Illnesses

Generally, chronic diseases reduce the quality of life, increase stress, increase the loss of productivity, and increase healthcare costs (some exceptions such as Canada due to universal healthcare) (Merdosy et al., 2020). Common factors that result in chronic illness among the homeless population are substance abuse, mental illness, exposure to a poor environment, poor sleeping and eating conditions, increased exposure to violence, and social stigma (Merdosy et al., 2020). In comparison to the general population, the prevalence of conditions is higher among the homeless. For example, a survey concluded the following statistics: arthritis and back pain are twice as common in the homeless population, migraine headaches are 3.5 times more prevalent, asthma is 3 times more common, and COPD is 4 times more common (Nikoo et al., 2015). In addition, diabetes mellitus reported in the homeless is half of the reported cases in the general population (Nikoo et al., 2015). Also, cancer is 1/8 more common in the homeless than in the general population (Nikoo et al., 2015). Also, 89% of the participants in a study under the age of 24 have self-reported at least one chronic health condition (Nikoo et al., 2015). White and Aboriginal ethnicities considerably reported long-term conditions such as diabetes mellitus and anemia (Nikoo et al., 2015). Some of the chronic illnesses that homeless people commonly experience are seizures, chronic obstructive pulmonary disease (COPD), arthritis, and other musculoskeletal disorders. Other conditions that are not controlled are hypertension, diabetes and anemia (Homeless Hub).

Mental Illnesses

Substance use disorder has high comorbidity with mental illness, especially in the homeless community (Jones et al., 2020). Recent epidemiological studies demonstrated that acute episodes of substance-induced psychosis can worsen to chronic psychotic disorders such as schizophrenia (Jones et al., 2020). Acute substance psychosis can be induced with substances such as methamphetamine, cocaine, cannabis and alcohol (Jones et al., 2020). Traumatic brain injury (TBI) is also associated with psychotic symptoms such as delusions and hallucinations (Jones et al., 2020). Substances highly associated with psychotic features were methamphetamine, alcohol and cannabis (Jones et al., 2020). In recent epidemiological studies, alcohol-induced psychosis was the most prevalent type of substance-induced psychosis (Jones et al., 2020). However, it was the least type of psychosis that was associated with the later diagnosis of schizophrenia (Jones et al., 2020). In recent epidemiological studies, cannabis and methamphetamine-induced psychosis are significantly correlated with the later development of schizophrenia or other persistent psychotic disorders (Jones et al., 2020).

In the late 1900s, the homelessness and association of mental disorders have increased due to the closure of psychiatric institutions (Institute of Medicine (U.S.). Committee on Health Care for Homeless People [IMCHCHP], 1988). A study conducted by Jones et al. (2020) revealed that psychotic features were prevalent in Vancouver, Canada. People are expected to have a high risk for suffering from mental illnesses when a history of psychotic disorder was diagnosed (Jones et al., 2020). Homeless people have a high risk of mental illness (IMCHCHP, 1988). Vice versa, mental illness can result in homelessness (IMCHCHP, 1988). Mental illnesses can exacerbate the ability to function and cope with surroundings or for others to cope with the behaviour of the person experiencing mental illness (IMCHCHP, 1988).

Personality disorders affect daily activities (IMCHCHP, 1988). It affects a person's ability to cope with regular functions and fit societal norms (IMCHCHP, 1988). It may be a contributing factor to homelessness but is not a cause of homelessness (IMCHCHP, 1988).

Neurological diseases

A study conducted in British Columbia in 2009 by Nikoo and others (2015) revealed that neurological diseases (72.60%) were highest in prevalence. TBI is the most prevalent neurological condition (Nikoo et al., 2015). TBI is reported to have a prevalence of 50% (Jones et al., 2020). Migraine headaches (29.2%) were the second-highest neurological condition reported (Nikoo et al., 2015). Some of the factors that cause chronic migraine are head injury, stressful life events, socioeconomic status and depression (Nikoo et al., 2015). These factors are prevalent in the homeless population (Nikoo et al., 2015). Therefore, migraines are common in people with homelessness.

Musculoskeletal diseases

Musculoskeletal diseases (52.20%) are the second-highest category of diseases that are prevalent in the homeless population (Nikoo et al., 2015). Some of the risk factors contributing to musculoskeletal problems are cognitive deficit, smoking, low education, low income, excessive alcohol consumption, depression, and anxiety (Nikoo et al., 2015).

Respiratory diseases

The prevalence rate of respiratory diseases is 31.80% (Nikoo et al., 2015). Respiratory diseases, such as asthma and COPD, are the most reported respiratory problems (Nikoo et al., 2015). A study in the US discovered that in 2002, homeless people were more than twice likely to have COPD compared to the general population (Nikoo et al., 2015). COPD is expected in the homeless because of a high incidence of smoking, poor nutrition, and adverse environmental exposure (Nikoo et al., 2015). Two other reports found a high frequency of cases of asthma in the homeless population (Nikoo et al., 2015). Asthma in homeless people is prevalent because of high cases of respiratory infections, smoking or second-hand smoking (Nikoo et al., 2015).

Cardiovascular diseases

In the same study of 500 homeless people by Nikoo and others (2015), 19.40% of homeless reported having cardiovascular disease. Cardiovascular diseases are the primary cause of mortality in the homeless population (Nikoo et al., 2015). The study conducted by Nikoo and others stated that 1/5 of the homeless people in this study have reported having cardiovascular disease (Nikoo et al., 2015). Even though hypertension is not found to have a high prevalence in the homeless community, however, it was found that there was a high prevalence of poor control of hypertension (Nikoo et al., 2015). Some factors of high risk of cardiovascular disease are emotional stress and high incidence of smoking (Nikoo et al., 2015). 60% of the deaths due to ischemic heart disease were associated with the use of tobacco (Baggett et al., 2018). About 1/4 of the recent cocaine users experiencing homelessness also experience cardiovascular diseases, such as atherosclerosis, myocardial ischemia and infarction, and other cardiac problems such as aortic dissection and sudden cardiac death due to drug overdose (Baggett et al., 2018). Also, post-traumatic stress disorder (PTSD) is greatly associated with cardiovascular disease. PTSD is estimated to impact 21% to 31% of homeless people (Baggett et al., 2018).

Diabetes

Conditions such as hypertension, anemia, and especially diabetes require self-management and adequate doses of medications regularly. However, there is a lack of self-management in people experiencing homelessness (Grewal et al., 2020). As a result, homeless people who have diabetes have poor glycemic control (Grewal et al., 2020). Poor glycemic control leads to harmful effects such as stroke, high risk of infections and heart failures. Also, people with diabetes require daily insulin injections, and control of diet is essential (IMCHCHP, 1988). However, for homeless people, this need is not met. Insulin requires cold temperatures and the usage of syringes (IMCHCHP, 1988). Nevertheless, syringes are stolen because IV drug abuse is common in the homeless population (IMCHCHP, 1988). It is not possible to have refrigerators. Also, diet cannot be controlled as homeless shelters cook whatever they are provided (IMCHCHP, 1988).

Traumatic disorders

Traumatic disorders are more common in homeless people than in the general population. Contusions, lacerations, sprains, bruises, and superficial burns are the most common traumatic injuries (IMCHCHP, 1988). The homeless population is at high risk for traumatic injuries because they are frequent victims of rape, assault, and attempted robbery (IMCHCHP, 1988). In addition, recent trauma is also linked with psychotic features or vice versa; People with psychotic features were susceptible to traumatic experiences (Jones et al., 2020).

Disorder of Skin and Blood vessels

Pustular skin lesions, usually a result of insect bites, and other infestations are frequent among the homeless (IMCHCHP, 1988). People experiencing homelessness also have poor circulation in the body because of extended periods of sitting or sleeping with their legs down (IMCHCHP, 1988). Also, swelling feet causes edema, cellulitis, and skin ulcerations. Recurrent dermatitis - a cause of unsanitary conditions, such as lack of bathe or showers - is associated with lice and scabies infestations (IMCHCHP, 1988). Lice and scabies are prevalent within the homeless population. In addition, they also have an increased chance of developing subcutaneous abscesses (IMCHCHP, 1988).

Other diseases

Other health problems commonly observed in homeless people are malnutrition, parasitic infestations, dental and periodontal disease, degenerative joint diseases, venereal diseases, hepatic cirrhosis secondary to alcoholism, and infectious hepatitis-related intravenous drug abuse (IMCHCHP, 1988). In addition, foot problems are at greater risk among homeless people. Some of the foot problems are fungal infections, calluses, corns, and bunions (IMCHCHP, 1988). They also suffer from poor dental care (IMCHCHP, 1988). Some dental problems are poor oral hygiene, cavities, gingival disease, and extractions with no prosthetic replacements (IMCHCHP, 1988).

Mortality

The mortality rates are higher in the homeless population compared to the general population. Compared to the general population of Montreal, the mortality rates of homeless youths are 9 times higher for males and 31 times higher for females (Frankish et al., 2005). Compared to the general population of Toronto, men in homeless shelters are two to eight times more likely to die (Frankish et al., 2005). A meta-analysis review by Aldridge and others (2018) suggests that SMRs (standard mortality ratios) are higher in females than males in the analyzed disease categories. SMR is calculated by dividing the observed number of deaths by the expected number of deaths (Patten, 2017).

Alcohol and drug dependence or abuse increases the mortality rate. Specifically, alcohol dependence and hepatic fibrosis increase the mortality rate (Jones et al., 2020). Psychotic disorders increase the risk of mortality (Jones et al., 2020). Homeless people under the age of 55 with a past psychotic disorder had an increased mortality risk (Jones et al., 2020). The alcohol-induced psychotic disorder is reported to have a high mortality risk (Jones et al., 2020). Circulatory diseases are the second leading cause of death (Baggett et al., 2018). Cardiovascular causes in the homeless population are between 61% to 71% (Baggett et al., 2018). Ischemia heart disease has a mortality rate of 63% to 80% (Baggett et al., 2018). Some environmental illnesses that increase the mortality of homeless people are hypothermia and frostbite (IMCHCHP, 1988).

Conclusion

People experiencing homelessness are increasing every year. The homeless population is more prevalent to chronic illnesses compared to the general population. Some illnesses that are prevalent in homeless people are mental illness, neurological diseases, musculoskeletal diseases, respiratory diseases, cardiovascular diseases, diabetes, traumatic disorders, the disorder of skin and blood vessels, and other problems. Also, homeless people have a high rate of mortality compared to housed people. Alcohol dependence, psychotic disorders, hypothermia, and frostbite increases mortality.

Chapter 10:

Effect of homelessness on addiction

Cassandra Van Drunen

Introduction

Homelessness and addiction are two intertwined subjects. In the year 2019, the US Department of Housing and Urban Development (HUD) reported that 567 715 individuals in the United States of America were either sleeping on the streets, in emergency shelters, or in transitional housing (Lautieri, 2019). From these chronically homeless individuals, the HUD believes that 36% have a chronic substance abuse problem, a severe mental illness, or both (Lautieri, 2019). Additionally, drug use is believed to be an integral component of the poor health and increased mortality risk that has been seen in various homeless communities (Grinman et al., 2010). Different subgroups of the homeless population, including women, indigenous individuals, and members of the LGBTQ+, are substantially different in terms of their relation and required intervention for addiction (Schütz, 2016). This chapter will explore the data and research regarding homelessness and addiction, on both a general and subgroup-specific scale.

Homelessness and Addiction in the General Population

The relationship between homelessness and addiction in general has been widely researched and discussed. Additionally, while this chapter is entitled "Effect of homelessness on addiction", the publication presented by Lautieri states it best that "substance abuse can be both the cause and result of homelessness" (Lautieri, 2019). This is an important consideration to remember while discussing the relationship between homelessness and addiction. There are two general theories that can be used to describe the relationship between homelessness and addiction: social selection and social causation (Pankratz & Pankratz, 2007).
In social selection, substance use leads individuals "to the streets" (Pankratz & Pankratz, 2007). Pankratz & Pankratz found research to back this model up that states that up to two thirds of homeless people claim alcohol and/or other drugs as a major or primary reason for being

homeless (Pankratz & Pankratz, 2007). Conversely, in social causation, "street life" increases substance use (Pankratz & Pankratz, 2007). There is also evidence that backs up this model linking the two topics, including data from the United Kingdom that stated 80% of respondents had started using at least one new drug since becoming homeless (Pankratz & Pankratz, 2007).

Many studies have worked to outline the prevalence of addiction within homeless populations in various locations, finding different results. One study made up of 500 individuals from British Columbia, who were either living on the street or in a homeless shelter, found that 78%, or 390 of those individuals suffered from at least one substance use disorder (excluding the use of tobacco) (Schütz, 2016). They also discovered that 68%, or 340 of the individuals had at least one mental disorder such as PTSD or depression and that 55%, or 275 of the people in the sample suffered from both substance abuse and mental disorders (Schütz, 2016). Additionally, alcohol problems within the past 30 days were present in 45% of those with current drug problems while conversely only 19% of those without current drug problems reported issues with alcohol (Schütz, 2016). Another interesting discovery was that of those with current drug issues within the past 30 days, only 27% stated that the drug and/or alcohol use was a component of their inability to get out of homelessness (Schütz, 2016). A different study based out of Toronto uncovered differing results (Grinman et al., 2010). This study by Grinman et al. that included 1191 homeless individuals found that the lifetime prevalence of the regular use of at least one type of drug was 60%, or 712 individuals (Grinman et al., 2010). Interestingly, 40%, or 475 individuals reported having a current drug use problem within the last 30 days (Ginman et al., 2010). A third report completed by the Government of Canada found that after surveying 19 536 people across 61 communities, the amount of individuals who suffer from addiction or substance use disorders will increase with the time they spent homeless (Quayum et al., 2021). This ranged from 19.0% in the individuals who had been homeless for 0-2 months of the year in 2018 to 28.2% in the individuals who had been homeless for 6 months or more (Quayum et al., 2021).

Now, what type of drugs are currently being abused most frequently? In the Toronto based study, researchers found that in the past two years, the most commonly abused drugs included were marijuana (40%), cocaine (27%), and opiate analgesics that were not either heroin or methadone (8%) (Grinman et al., 2010). In terms of present drug use (within the last 30 days), marijuana and cocaine remained the two highest reported drugs (Grinman et al., 2010). Conversely, according to the American Addiction Centers, the three most commonly abused drug groups among the homeless population, besides alcohol, include heroin and prescription opiates, methamphetamine, and cocaine (Lautieri, 2021).

Homeless Women Versus Men and Addiction

Are there differences between homeless men and women in terms of addiction? Some sources would agree. Referring back to the Toronto based study by Grinman et al., they found that the prevalence of current drug problems within the study group varied between both genders and if the adult had dependents (Grinman et al., 2010). The rate of prevalence in single men was 53% as opposed to 41% in single women and the even smaller fraction of 12% in adults with children (Grinman et al., 2010). The study also stated that homeless individuals with drug use problems were significantly more likely to be "single men, white, Canadian-born, and lacking a high school degree" as well as more likely to have been both younger and homeless at a younger age (Grinman et al., 2010). Additionally, there were differences when it came to the abuse of specific drugs within a two year period (Grinman et al., 2010). Marijuana use was reported in 51% of single men and 35% of single women whereas cocaine was 32% for both demographics (Grinman et al., 2010). This study however was not the only one to notice a difference in these two subgroups. In the aforementioned study completed by the Government of Canada, men were more likely to blame addiction and substance use as a reason for their housing loss, coming in at 27.6% as opposed to women's 21.0% and gender diverse individuals coming in at 22.7% (Quayum et al., 2021). Flying over to Australia, a 2016-2017 annual report found that 288 000 people assisted by specialist homlessness services, nearly 9% of the homeless individuals, identified as having drug use problems and/or suffering from alcohol abuse (Thomas & Menih, 2021).

Looking at women specifically, a study by Groton and Radey examined how social networks of homeless women affected their homelessness, touching also on the link to substance abuse. They found in their discussions with 20 women that "network substance abuse" can contribute to the homelessness experienced by women (Groton & Radey, 2019). The women from this group described using different substances from a young age by modeling behaviour from older siblings while others explained that they began to abuse substances to deal with their abusive relationships as grown adults (Groton & Radey, 2019). One woman specifically described to the research team how her abusive relationship led to her substance abuse: "So, when I go and move in with him, right there, bam—just beat me so bad. So, I'm just miserable. I'm depressed, like, I didn't have the cure—like, get some type of drug– that's when I got hooked on marijuana. So then I just started smoking marijuana, like heavy, back to back.... I stay smoking weed but it was cuz, like, I needed to numb my pain" (Groton & Radey, 2019). Gorton and Radey also discussed how substance abuse in other's can impact women exiting homelessness, specifically slowing it down (Gorton and Radey, 2019). One woman from the study discussed how her partner's chronic substance abuse caused her to have damaged property and slowed down her overall path out of homelessness: "my dad, when we were in [city] kept having to send me a new phone. And, like, he'd have to call [phone company] like every 3 weeks cuz he'd [boyfriend] get paranoid and think the thing [phone] was looking at him and take a screwdriver to the camera part of it and stab the thing. And so now I've had to set boundaries" (Gorton and Radey, 2019). Even though she had support from her father, her boyfriend's actions greatly impacted her ability to end her homelessness (Gorton and Radey, 2019).

Homeless Youth and Addiction

In Canada, it is estimated that approximately 6000 youth between the ages of 15 and 25 are homeless every night (Doré-Gauthier et al., 2019). Staggeringly, the estimated rates of substance use and addiction for homeless youth are significantly high. While Addiction Center cites that 71% of missing, runaway, throwaway, or abducted children have been reported to struggle with substance abuse disorder, other reports have estimated that the number is slightly higher at 75% (Murray & Hampton, 2021; Doré-Gauthier et al., 2019). Additionally, according to the aforementioned report completed by the Government of Canada, of those reporting addiction or substance use, 23.7% were youth between the ages of 13 and 24, the second highest category behind the 28.2% of adults aged 25-49 (Quayum et al., 2021). In terms of drug choice, marijuana has been deemed the "drug of choice" for homeless youth (Gomez et al., 2010). Additionally, cocaine has been determined to be 4 to 5 times more likely to be abused in homeless youth compared to their house counterparts while amphetamine use is 3 to 4 times more likely to be abused (Gomez et al., 2010).

Getting away from the numbers, there are many factors that can be considered that contribute to youth homeless substance abuse and that aid or hinder transitions in and out of youth homelessness. Addiction Center lists eight factors that can contribute to youth homeless substance abuse which include growing up in a homeless family, genetics of substance abuse, family abuse, maladaptive coping mechanism for stress, co-occurring disorders, early use of substances, physical, sexual and emotional abuse, and finally running away from home (Murray & Hampton, 2021). Additionally, homeless youth who have substance use problems are significantly more likely to have long-term substance abuse issues and untreated co-occuring disorder that follow them into their adult years (Murray & Hampton, 2021). A different study of 685 drug-using youth between the ages of 14 and 26 helped uncover factors that can affect youths transitions into and out of homelessness (Cheng et al., 2013). The team concluded that access to addiction treatment services, housing availability, exposure to the criminal justice system, and employment opportunities all were factors that were correlated to transitions into and out of homelessness (Cheng et al., 2013).

Homeless Indigenous Individuals and Addiction

The misuse of substances and homelessness are intertwined results for Indigenous people who have suffered through the intergenerational trauma that was caused by the Canadian residential school system and the 60's Scoop (Victor et al., 2019). While minimal data could be found regarding homeless Native individuals and addiction compared to other demographics, some interesting discoveries were found. In the report by the Government of Canada, those who identified as Indigenous were similarly as likely to report addiction and substance use as the reason for their housing loss (27.7%) compared to their non-Indigenous counterparts (27.2%) (Quayum et al., 2021). Additionally, when focusing in on the Indigenous individuals, First Nations (28.5%) and Métis (28.4%) individuals were slightly more likely to cite addiction and substance use as the reason for their lack of housing than Inuit (24.4%) individuals and those with Indigenous ancestry (24.1%) (Quayum et al., 2021). Interestingly, there are differences in these statistics when comparing Indigenous men and women (Quayum et al., 2021). Women who identified as Indigienous were more likely to report addiction and substance use as their reason for lost housing than non-Indigenous women (27.9% v.s. 21.4%) while Indigenous men were less likely than their non-Indigenous male counterparts (27.8% v.s. 30.0%) (Quayum et al., 2021). Additionally, an interesting study on Indigenous youth specifically found that Indigenous youth had greater mental health and addiction challenges than their non-Indigenous youth counterparts (Kidd et al., 2019). This study also recognized that it is not simply a physical home that is affecting Indigenous individuals but "stable cultural and social matrixes" (Kidd et al., 2019).

Homeless LGBTQ+ Individuals and Addiction

Homeless LGBTQ+ individuals face their own struggles compared to other demographics. In fact, LGBTQ+ community members have a 120% higher risk of ending up homeless (Murray & Hampton, 2021). Additionally, according to Psychology Today, this demographic "have the highest number of illicit drug use" (Murray & Hampton, 2021). There are several factors that contribute to the trends of homelessness and addiction in the LGBTQ+ community (Hull, 2020). Many of the members of this community have shared life experiences of familial rejection, abuse and neglect, which are drivers of homelessness and risk factors for addiction (Hull, 2020).

A specific study performed to find the pathways to homelessness in the LGBTQ+ demographic (Ecker et al., 2020). This study found that 50% of their study group, which was composed of 20 people, stated that substance abuse was a contributing factor to their homelessness (Ecker et al., 2020). In fact, some listed it as the sole reason for their homelessness, including one cisgneder bisexual man who stated ""Entry into homelessness? The addiction. One hundred percent. No doubt about it." (Ecker et al., 2020). They also found the substance abuse was mostly stated to predate their homelessness rather than being a consequence of this demographic homelessness (Ecker et al., 2020). Additionally, one homeless individual stated that his descent into addiction was due to being uncomfortable with his sexuality (Ecker et al., 2020). He elaborated that "I'm in this part of my life right now, I'm struggling with myself. It's not because only my drug addiction make me like that, okay? It's because I realize before, but I don't want to go through it, I can't accept myself about being gay" (Ecker et al., 2020).

Number From Other Demographics

When the Government of Canada completed their report on addiction, substance use, and homelessness, they included results from other demographics that were interesting to analyze (Quayum et al., 2021). For example, Immigrants (11.4%), , refugees (7.9%), or refugee claimants (3.3%) were less likely to state that addiction and substance use was a contributing factor to their homelessness when compared to non-newcomers (Quayum et al., 2021). Additionally, just like the new-comers demographic, veterans (19.0%) were less likely to say that addiction and substance use was a factor contributing to their homelessness than non-veterans (25.4%) (Quayum et al., 2021).

Conclusion

In conclusion, there is a strong link between homelessness and addiction, and this link is different across various demographics. These individuals require different aids and healthcare strategies to combat their addictions and substance use disorders. Additionally, many of these subgroups and minority demographics deserve more attention from research teams so that the barriers to their required healthcare can continue to be knocked down. As time moves on, we should hope to see the numbers of addiction in homeless communities decrease as healthcare becomes more accessible to them.

Chapter 11:

Public Initiatives seeking to address barriers to accessible healthcare

Angelin Valancia Thipahar

Introduction

After reading about the breadth of the issue, the question that remains is, what has been done to alleviate the burden of illness from this population? Currently, government interventions which focus on addressing these many obstacles have been implemented and the conversation around equitable healthcare is ongoing. Governments have, under the threat of COVID-19, realized that there are healthcare policies in need of revision. Non-governmental organizations (NGOs) that have focused on implementing equitable healthcare for vulnerable populations have also made strides forward to achieve this. The hope for the homeless population is that, with the right intervention, individuals will not have to have their low socio-economic status be synonymous with a lower standard of living. The hope for everyone is that this conversation of equitable healthcare is kept as a priority even after the effects of the pandemic diminish but, that is a topic for another book. From previous chapters, you may have already understood that eliminating the barriers to accessible healthcare for the homeless is a multi-faceted endeavour. Generally, people that live in low socio-economic conditions are more susceptible to illness and, often, have fewer resources available to them. However, the issue is made more complex by the fact that homeless populations are more likely to fall prey to poor mental health, addiction to substances, and infectious diseases. The social climate and the less than optimal environment that these individuals are placed in increases the severity of the issue as well. How can governments and/or NGOs fix such a layered issue? Within this chapter, we will be discussing the new interventions that have surfaced as a result of the COVID-19 pandemic, the effectiveness of this intervention and the importance of considering the policy literature on the subject going forward.

COVID-19: Creating an Urgent Need for Accessible Healthcare

COVID-19 has certainly redefined our understanding of the health care sector. Suddenly, the differences in healthcare accessibility for those experiencing homelessness and the general population have become staggeringly obvious. Public Health Ontario conducted an environmental scan in 2021 wherein actions, both short and intermediate term, to meet the basic health and social needs for the homeless population were identified. Homelessness in Canada is a layered issue with a plethora of underlying causes that are being addressed from a federal, provincial and organizational level. Which is why, it should be noted that, while this report provides a broad spectrum of current intervention, it is not all-encompassing. The government has been implementing several strategies to alleviate the burden of the pandemic for the homeless population. These strategies work towards eradicating the barriers for accessible healthcare for this population. As learned from Chapter 4, housing and environmental concerns in homeless shelters, lowered access to mental health and counselling resources, and worry over the level of food security are factors that serve to diminish the health of people who are experiencing homelessness. These social determinants are currently being addressed.

To provide improved housing conditions, the government has supported the addition of new shelter spaces which allow for greater maintenance of physical distancing and reduction of the risk for COVID-19 transmission in shelters. Several jurisdictions within Canada used vacant hotel/motel rooms, government buildings, and office buildings to house the homeless. It goes without saying that the COVID-19 enforced isolation poses risk to people experiencing homelessness. The Canadian government has attempted to curb the adverse effects of lowered access to mental health and substance use needs by providing homeless populations with counselling services, substance use case management/harm reduction services, opioid therapy, and enhanced needle collection service. Strategies to improve the environment in already existing shelters are also underway. These interventions include social distancing, cleaning protocols, staggered meal times and usage of common areas, delivering meals, halting social activities, restricting shower and laundry facilities, and adding security to enforce physical distancing rules (City of Toronto, 2020). To allow those who do not frequent shelters better accessibility to proper hygiene, portable washrooms and handwashing stations were situated in various areas within several cities. Similar facilities to these as well as showers and water fountains are also available in park areas. Nova Scotia, Ontario and British Columbia have, additionally, provided support towards food banks and have funded food security measures.

Several of the non-governmental organizations listed in the environmental scan had the Indigenous homeless population at the forefront of their endeavours. This is due to the fact that there is a gross overrepresentation of this minority group amid the homeless population of Canada.

In London, Ontario, an indigenous housing hub supported by an outreach team enables homeless individuals belonging to this minority to learn about and reconnect with their culture (Richmond & Stacey, 2020). The housing hub has ten resting spaces meaning that it is intervention on a smaller scale, however, it is making a difference all the same. In Montreal, Quebec, a sports centre provides 40 beds, hot meals, showers, cleaning staff and intervention workers such as nurses to aid the Indigenous community (Fennario, 2020). The centre also accommodates individuals using substances who may not be accepted into other shelters. This particular shelter is open 24-hours which increases the likelihood that those who inhabit it will remain stagnant for a longer period of time. In Manitoba, an organization called Keewatinowi Okimakanak Inc. gave the YWCA Thompson hostel the necessary funding to continue housing First Nations people (Sandberg,

2020). Through this funding, the YWCA was able to enforce physical distancing, screening, and hand-washing practices. The hostel also provided masks, gloves, and access to laundry and shower facilities. The Indigenous organization, Anishnawbe Health Toronto converted a recreational vehicle into a mobile health service for the First Nations people experiencing homelessness within Toronto. This NGO provides health care, COVID-19 testing and temporary housing accommodations.

Effectiveness of Intervention

Now, from these lists of interventions, it seems as though Canada is being quite effective at managing those experiencing homelessness over the course of the pandemic. But, is this really the case? Before the onset of the pandemic, the issue of homelessness had not garnered the same amount of attention as it has today. A research report which focused on the insights of young people who had previously experienced being homeless offers perspective as to what policymakers should be considering when creating policies for this group (Gaetz et al, 2018). The report addresses the futility of a crisis-based approach to solving youth homelessness and how several opportunities to prevent youth homelessness within public systems are not explored. Emergency responses to issues the homeless population contend with does little to help individuals exit their current situation.

While not all of the current intervention taking place to aid the homeless population is a reactive response to the pandemic, the fact remains that several measures are only in place due to the current global situation. Even amid these measures, 74 people living in Toronto shelters have died over the past year (Gibson, 2021). This is a 54% increase from the death toll among shelter residents in 2019. What is perhaps most upsetting about this statistic is only 7% of the deaths were COVID-19 related. 25% of deaths recorded from January to July of 2020 were due to drug toxicity. Looking at overall deaths for the sheltered homeless population, 10% were a result of cardiovascular disease, 2% were cancer-related, 3% were due to pneumonia, 2% were homicides, 3% were suicides, and 47% of the deaths do not yet have a definitive cause (Gibson, 2021).

The intervention provided over the course of COVID-19 was successful in curbing the spread of COVID. Its effectiveness at addressing the barriers to healthcare that homeless individuals face could be improved. While the option of being housed is undoubtedly preferable to braving the harsh outside environment, the fact remains that people experiencing homeless are more susceptible to mental illness and substance addiction. Their new isolated accommodations create an environment that is not conducive to these issues. During the pandemic, in Ontario, more people died as a result of an overdose compared to prior years. The homeless population requires policies that work towards addressing the root causes for the barriers to healthcare. These policies cannot simply be responses to adverse conditions that temporarily fix the problem. Long term solutions that are sustainable and cater to the needs of each subpopulation within the homeless community are required.

Creating Policies That Address the Multi-Faceted Nature of Homelessness

These strategies are not enough to address the issue of inequity in healthcare for people who experience homelessness. The manner in which society has dealt with this problem has been reactive rather than proactive (Gaetz et al., 2018). Interventions going forward should pay heed to the scientific literature which seeks to better understand the manner in which social determinants of health factor into policymaking. For example, a systematic review conducted by Formosa et al. addresses how emergency department (ED) interventions can be highly effective for improving the social determinants of health for homeless individuals (2020). Most of the homeless population use ED as their primary means of accessing healthcare and are then discharged back into homelessness. In this paper, the idea of ED as a means of establishing housing and addressing variables related to substance use and access to primary care is discussed.

Included in this review are two housing first initiatives which successfully housed patients and, simultaneously, addressed their social determinants of health (Formosa et al., 2020). Housing first initiatives provide immediate access to mental health support services and rent supplements. Traditionally, homeless individuals are required to stop using substances or receive psychiatric treatment before they are deemed eligible for housing support services (CAMH, 2019). This creates an incentive for people experiencing homelessness to actively seek help for their mental health issues and substance use needs. Diamant et al. tracked the level of care that homeless individuals received within their housing first study and noticed that a significantly higher degree of patients with a familiarized source of healthcare (2011). As well, they noticed a decline in the amount of patients that typically opted out of much needed medical care. Creating proper incentives clearly produces results. Another study within this systematic review (Formosa et al., 2020), spearheaded by McCormack and DeMuth in 2016, targeted substance use disorder directly. Substance use disorder can contribute to housing loss, cause difficulty in maintaining stable living accommodations, and is often linked to other issues faced by the homeless population. The study focused on using naltrexone (an opiate substitute) in combination with concurrent case management — a short term intensive case management program for those struggling with both mental and substance use issues (McCormack & DeMuth, 2016). The results of the study were quite promising.

The reason why the same measures utilized within these studies might not be reflected within government policies is, again, due to all the other factors that must be considered, for example, the demographics of the homeless populations in different regions in Canada. As the issue at hand is multi-faceted, its solution must be multi-faceted and cater to specific requirements of the subsects of the homeless population.

Through the previous chapters that outline the different experiences that people who are homeless face, it would be presumptuous to assume that the same intervention that succeeds within one subsect of this population will work for everyone. However, studies like the ones cited here and within the previous chapters of this book further the conversation toward effective change. The greater the awareness given to presenting various homeless populations with proper care and the more we remain committed to achieving equitable healthcare, the sooner we will be able to eradicate the issues created by homelessness altogether.

Conclusion

On any given night, at least 35,000 Canadians are experiencing homelessness. While access to shelter and food are often the primary concern for these individuals, healthcare is often a prominent yet overlooked issue. From vulnerability to infectious diseases to addiction and mental health, the homeless population is consistently disadvantaged when accessing treatment for a wide spectrum of conditions. Given the devastating impact these barriers have on individuals' health, sustained collaborative effort is crucial if we hope to curtail the impact of this issue in the future.

References

Chapter 1

Gaetz, S., Barr, C., Friesen, A., Harris, B., Hill, C., Kovacs-Burns, K., Pauly, B., Pearce, B., Turner, A., & Marsolais, A. (2012). Canadian Definition of Homelessness.

Gaetz, S., Dej, E., Richter, T., & Redman, M. (2016). The State of Homelessness in Canada 2016. www.homelesshub.ca

Gaetz, S., Donaldson, J., Richter, T., Gulliver, T., Gaetz, S. ;, Donaldson, J. ;, Richter, T. ;, & Vasko, S. (2013). The State of Homelessness in Canada 2013 How to cite this document. www.homelesshub.ca

Gaetz, S., Donaldson, J., Richter, T., Gulliver, T., & Vasko, S. (2013). The State of Homelessness in Canada 2013 How to cite this document. www.homelesshub.ca

Government of Canada. (n.d.). What Is the Strategy? | A Place to Call Home. Retrieved July 13, 2021, from https://www.placetocallhome.ca/what-is-the-strategy

Statistics Canada. (2014). Shelters for abused women in Canada, 2014. https://www150.statcan.gc.ca/n1/pub/85-002-x/2015001/article/14207-eng.htm

Statistics Canada. (2016). Census of Population, 2016 - Core housing need. https://www12.statcan.gc.ca/census-recensement/2016/ref/dict/households-menage037-eng.cfm

The Homeless Hub. (n.d.-a). Addressing Chronic Homelessness | The Homeless Hub. Retrieved July 13, 2021, from https://www.homelesshub.ca/solutions/prevention/addressing-chronic-homelessness

The Homeless Hub. (n.d.-b). Domestic Violence & Homelessness | The Homeless Hub. Retrieved July 13, 2021, from https://www.homelesshub.ca/blog/domestic-violence-homelessness

The Homeless Hub. (n.d.-c). How many people are homeless in Canada? | The Homeless Hub. Retrieved July 13, 2021, from https://www.homelesshub.ca/about-homelessness/homelessness-101/how-many-people-are-homeless-canada

The Homeless Hub. (n.d.-d). Substance Use & Addiction. Retrieved July 13, 2021, from https://www.homelesshub.ca/about-homelessness/topics/substance-use-addiction

Chapter 2

Campbell, D. J., O'Neill, B. G., Gibson, K., & Thurston, W. E. (2015). Primary healthcare needs and barriers to care among Calgary's homeless populations. BMC Family Practice, 16. https://doi.org/10.1186/s12875-015-0361-3

Government of Ontario. (n.d.). Ambulance Services Billing. Ministry of Health, Ministry of Longterm Care. https://www.health.gov.on.ca/en/public/publications/ohip/amb.aspx.

Gulliver, T. (2014). How Can We Improve Healthcare Access for the Homeless? How Can We Improve Healthcare Access for the Homeless? | The Homeless Hub. https://www.homelesshub.ca/resource/how-can-we-improve-healthcare-access-homeless.

Hwang, S. W. (2001). Homelessness and health. CMAJ, 164(2), 229–233.

Khandor, E., Mason, K., Chambers, C., Rossiter, K., Cowan, L., & Hwang, S. W. (2011). Access to primary health care among homeless adults in Toronto, Canada: results from the Street Health survey. Open medicine : a peer-reviewed, independent, open-access journal, 5(2), e94–e103.

Khatana, S. A., Wadhera, R. K., Choi, E., Groeneveld, P. W., Culhane, D. P., Kushel, M., Kazi, D. S., Yeh, R. W., & Shen, C. (2020). Association of Homelessness with Hospital Readmissions—an Analysis of Three Large States. Journal of General Internal Medicine, 35(9), 2576–2583. https://doi.org/10.1007/s11606-020-05946-4

Liu, M., & Hwang, S. W. (2021). Health care for homeless people. Nature Reviews Disease Primers, 7(1). https://doi.org/10.1038/s41572-020-00241-2

Ramsay, N., Hossain, R., Moore, M., Milo, M., & Brown, A. (2019). Health Care While Homeless: Barriers, Facilitators, and the Lived Experiences of Homeless Individuals Accessing Health Care in a Canadian Regional Municipality. Qualitative Health Research, 29(13), 1839–1849. https://doi.org/10.1177/1049732319829434

Shepherd, L. (2010). Toronto homeless report barriers to health care. Eurekalert.

Strobel, S., Burcul, I., Dai, J. H., Ma, Z., Jamani, S., & Hossein, R. (2021). Characterizing people experiencing homelessness and trends in homelessness using population-level emergency department visit data in Ontario, Canada. Statistics Canada. https://doi.org/10.25318/82-003-x202100100002-eng

Chapter 3

Campbell, David J. T., Braden G. O'Neill, Katherine Gibson, and Wilfreda E. Thurston. 2015. "Primary Healthcare Needs and Barriers to Care among Calgary's Homeless Populations." BMC Family Practice 2015 16:1 16(1): 1–10. https://bmcfampract.biomedcentral.com/articles/10.1186/s12875-015-0361-3 (July 15, 2021).

Liu, Michael, and Stephen W. Hwang. 2021. "Health Care for Homeless People." Nature Reviews Disease Primers 2021 7:1 7(1): 1–2. https://www.nature.com/articles/s41572-020-00241-2 (July 15, 2021).

Purkey, Eva, and Meredith MacKenzie. 2019. "Experience of Healthcare among the Homeless and Vulnerably Housed a Qualitative Study: Opportunities for Equity-Oriented Health Care." International Journal for Equity in Health 2019 18:1 18(1): 1–7. https://equityhealthj.biomedcentral.com/articles/10.1186/s12939-019-1004-4 (July 15, 2021).

Turnbull, Jeffrey, Wendy Muckle, and Christina Masters. 2007. "Homelessness and Health." Cmaj 177(9): 1065–66.

Chapter 4

Campbell, D.J.T., O'Neill, B.G., Gibson, K. et al. (2015). Primary healthcare needs and barriers to care among Calgary's homeless populations. BMC Fam Pract 16, 139. https://doi.org/10.1186/s12875-015-0361-3

Dorling, D., Mitchell, R., & Pearce, J. (2007). The global impact of income inequality on health by age: an observational study. BMJ, 335(7625), 873–875. https://doi.org/10.1136/bmj.39349.507315.DE

Gold, K. (2011). Analysis: the impact of needle, syringe, and lancet disposal on the community. Journal of Diabetes Science and Technology, 5(4), 848–850. https://doi.org/10.1177/193229681100500404

Hahn, R. A., & Truman, B. I. (2015). Education Improves Public Health and Promotes Health Equity. International Journal of Health Services, 45(4), 657–678. https://doi.org/10.1177/0020731415585986

Moffa, M., Cronk, R., Fejfar, D., Dancausse, S., Padilla, L. A., & Bartram, J. (2019). A systematic scoping review of environmental health conditions and hygiene behaviors in homeless shelters. International Journal of Hygiene and Environmental Health, 222(3), 335–346. https://doi.org/10.1016/j.ijheh.2018.12.004

Chapter 5

Howells, K., Burrows, M., Amp, M., Brennan, R., Yeung, W. L., Jackson, S., ... & Sanders, C. (2021). Exploring the experiences of changes to support access to primary health care services and the impact on the quality and safety of care for homeless people during the COVID-19 pandemic: a study protocol for a qualitative mixed methods approach. International Journal for Equity in Health, 20(1), 1-9. https://doi.org/10.1186/s12939-020-01364-4

Parkes, T., Carver, H., Masterton, W., Falzon, D., Dumbrell, J., Grant, S., & Wilson, I. (2021). "You know, we can change the services to suit the circumstances of what is happening in the world": a rapid case study of the COVID-19 response across city centre homelessness and health services in Edinburgh, Scotland. Harm reduction journal, 18(1), 1-18. https://doi.org/10.1186/s12954-021-00508-1

Şahin, A., Tasci, M., & Yan, J. (2020). The unemployment cost of COVID-19: How high and how long?. Economic commentary, (2020-09). https://ideas.repec.org/a/fip/fedcec/87920.html

Van Rüth, V., König, H. H., Bertram, F., Schmiedel, P., Ondruschka, B., Püschel, K., & Hajek, A. (2021). Determinants of health-related quality of life among homeless individuals during the COVID-19 pandemic. Public health, 194, 60-66. https://doi.org/10.1016/j.puhe.2021.02.026

Chapter 6

Beezhold, B., Radnitz, C., Rinne, A., & DiMatteo, J. (2014). Vegans report less stress and anxiety than omnivores. Nutritional Neuroscience, 18(7), 289-296. https://doi.org/10.1179/1476830514y.0000000164

Canada's Food Guide. Government of Canada. (2021). Retrieved 12 July 2021, from https://food-guide.canada.ca/en/.

D'andreamatteo, C., & Slater, J. (2018). Measuring Food Security in Canadian Homeless Adult Men. Canadian Journal Of Dietetic Practice And Research, 79(1), 42-45. https://doi.org/10.3148/cjdpr-2017-026

Holmes, R. (2018). RE: Malnutrition in Canadian hospitals. CMAJ. Retrieved 10 July 2021, from https://www.cmaj.ca/content/re-malnutrition-canadian-hospitals.

Household food insecurity in Canada statistics and graphics (2011 to 2012) - Canada.ca. Statistics Canada. (2020). Retrieved 10 July 2021, from https://www.canada.ca/en/health-canada/services/nutrition-science-research/food-security/household-food-security-statistics-2011-2012.html.

Koh, K., Hoy, J., O'Connell, J., & Montgomery, P. (2012). The Hunger–Obesity Paradox: Obesity in the Homeless. Journal Of Urban Health, 89(6), 952-964. https://doi.org/10.1007/s11524-012-9708-4

Lesani, A., Mohammadpoorasl, A., Javadi, M., Esfeh, J., & Fakhari, A. (2016). Eating breakfast, fruit and vegetable intake and their relation with happiness in college students. Eating And Weight Disorders - Studies On Anorexia, Bulimia And Obesity, 21(4), 645-651. https://doi.org/10.1007/s40519-016-0261-0

Li, A., Dachner, N., & Tarasuk, V. (2009). Food Intake Patterns of Homeless Youth in Toronto. Canadian Journal Of Public Health, 100(1), 36-40. https://doi.org/10.1007/bf03405490

Martins, D., Gorman, K., Miller, R., Murphy, L., Sor, S., Martins, J., & Vecchiarelli, M. (2015). Assessment of Food Intake, Obesity, and Health Risk among the Homeless in Rhode Island. Public Health Nursing, 32(5), 453-461. https://doi.org/10.1111/phn.12180

Mulik, K., & Haynes-Maslow, L. (2017). The Affordability of MyPlate: An Analysis of SNAP Benefits and the Actual Cost of Eating According to the Dietary Guidelines. Journal Of Nutrition Education And Behavior, 49(8), 623-631.e1. https://doi.org/10.1016/j.jneb.2017.06.005

Overweight and obese adults, 2018. Statistics Canada. (2019). Retrieved 8 July 2021, from https://www150.statcan.gc.ca/n1/pub/82-625-x/2019001/article/00005-eng.htm.

Poor diet | Food Policy for Canada. Foodpolicyforcanada.info.yorku.ca. Retrieved 15 July 2021, from https://foodpolicyforcanada.info.yorku.ca/backgrounder/problems/poor-diet/.

Salads or No, Cheap Burgers Revive McDonald's. Faculty.washington.edu. (2021). Retrieved 15 July 2021, from http://faculty.washington.edu/sundar/MM-BBUS320/Fun-READINGS/McDonalds.pdf.

Slater, J., & Mudryj, A. (2018). Are we really "eating well with Canada's food guide"?. BMC Public Health, 18(1). https://doi.org/10.1186/s12889-018-5540-4

Slavin, J., & Lloyd, B. (2012). Health Benefits of Fruits and Vegetables. Advances In Nutrition, 3(4), 506-516. https://doi.org/10.3945/an.112.002154

Tsai, J., & Rosenheck, R. A. (2013). Obesity among Chronically Homeless Adults: Is it a Problem? Public Health Reports, 128(1), 29–36. https://doi.org/10.1177/003335491312800105

Westhoek, H., Lesschen, J., Rood, T., Wagner, S., De Marco, A., & Murphy-Bokern, D. et al. (2014). Food choices, health and environment: Effects of cutting Europe's meat and dairy intake. Global Environmental Change, 26, 196-205. https://doi.org/10.1016/j.gloenvcha.2014.02.004

World Health Organization (2015). Diet, nutrition and the prevention of chronic diseases: Report of the joint WHO/FAO expert consultation. http://www.who.int/dietphysicalactivity/publications/trs916/summary/en/

Chapter 7

Aleman. (2016). Infectious Diseases | The Homeless Hub. Retrieved from https://www.homelesshub.ca/blog/infectious-diseases

Badiaga, S., Raoult, D., & Brouqui, P. (2008). Preventing and Controlling Emerging and Reemerging Transmissible Diseases in the Homeless. Emerging Infectious Diseases, 14(9), 1353–1359. https://doi.org/10.3201/eid1409.082042

Leung, C. S., Ho, M. M., Kiss, A., Gundlapalli, A. V., & Hwang, S. W. (2008). Homelessness and the Response to Emerging Infectious Disease Outbreaks: Lessons from SARS. Journal of Urban Health, 85(3), 402–410. https://doi.org/10.1007/s11524-008-9270-2

Ng, J., Sutherland, C., & Kolber, M. R. (2017). Does evidence support supervised injection sites? Canadian Family Physician, 63(11), 866.

State of Homelessness: 2020 Edition. (2020). National Alliance to End Homelessness. Retrieved from https://endhomelessness.org/homelessness-in-america/homelessness-statistics/state-of-homelessness-2020/

Wolitski, R. J., Kidder, D. P., & Fenton, K. A. (2007). HIV, Homelessness, and Public Health: Critical Issues and a Call for Increased Action. AIDS and Behavior, 11(2), 167. https://doi.org/10.1007/s10461-007-9277-9

Chapter 8

Azarmehr, H., Lowry, K., Sherman, A., Smith, C., & Zuñiga, J. A. (2018). Nursing Practice Strategies for Prenatal Care of Homeless Pregnant Women. Nursing for Women's Health, 22(6), 489–498. https://doi.org/10.1016/j.nwh.2018.09.005

Committee on Health Care for Homeless People. (1988). Health Care Services for Homeless People. Homelessness, Health, and Human Needs.

Corey, E., Frazin, S., Heywood, S., & Haider, S. (2020). Desire for and barriers to obtaining effective contraception among women experiencing homelessness. Contraception and Reproductive Medicine, 5(12). https://doi.org/10.1186/s40834-020-00113-w

Cronley, C., Hohn, K., & Nahar, S. (2017). Reproductive health rights and survival: The voices of mothers experiencing homelessness. Women & Health, 58(3), 320–333.

https://doi.org/10.1080/03630242.2017.1296060

Duchesne, A. (2015). Women and Homelessness in Canada: A brief review of the literature [dissertation]. McGill University.

Gelberg, L., Leake, B., Lu, M. C., Andersen, R. M., Nyamathi, A. M., Morgenstern, H., & Browner, C. (2002). Chronically Homeless Women's Perceived Deterrents to Contraception. Perspectives on Sexual and Reproductive Health, 34(6), 278–285. https://doi.org/10.2307/3097746

The Homeless Hub. (n.d.). Sexual/Reproductive Care. The Homeless Hub.

https://www.homelesshub.ca/about-homelessness/health/sexualreproductive-care.

House of Commons, & Casey, B., The Health of LGBTQIA2 Communities in Canada (2019). House of Commons.

Johnston-Robledo, I., & Chrisler, J. C. (2020). The Menstrual Mark: Menstruation as Social Stigma. The Palgrave Handbook of Critical Menstruation Studies, 181–199.

https://doi.org/10.1007/978-981-15-0614-7_17

Keohane, I. (2017, July 19). Homelessness, reproductive health & pregnancy. The Homeless Hub. https://www.homelesshub.ca/blog/homelessness-reproductive-health-pregnancy.

National Sexual Violence Resource Center. (n.d.) Homeless Youth & Sexual Violence [infographic]. National Sexual Violence Resource Center.

https://www.nsvrc.org/sites/default/files/publications/2019-02/HomelessYouth_Final%20 508.pdf

NCTE. (n.d.). Housing & Homelessness. National Center for Transgender Equality. https://transequality.org/issues/housing-homelessness.

Paisi, M., March-McDonald, J., Burns, L., Snelgrove-Clarke, E., Withers, L., & Shawe, J. (2020). Perceived barriers and facilitators to accessing and utilising sexual and reproductive healthcare for people who experience homelessness: a systematic review.

BMJ Sexual & Reproductive Health, 47(3), 211–220.

https://doi.org/10.1136/bmjsrh-2020-200799

Parrillo, A., & Feller, E. (2017). Menstrual hygiene plight of homeless women, a public health disgrace. Rhode Island Medical Journal, 100(12), 14–15.

http://www.rimed.org/rimedicaljournal/2017/12/2017-12-14-pov-parrillo.pdf.

Rak, A. (2018, May 17). Sexual and Reproductive Health and LGBTQ2S Youth Experiencing Homelessness. The Homeless Hub.

https://www.homelesshub.ca/blog/sexual-and-reproductive-health-and-lgbtq2s-youth-experiencing-homelessness.

Saver, B. G., Weinreb, L., Gelberg, L., & Zerger, S. (2012). Provision of Contraceptive Services to Homeless Women: Results of a Survey of Health Care for the Homeless Providers. Women & Health, 52(2), 151–161. https://doi.org/10.1080/03630242.2011.649829

Sommer, M., Gruer, C., Smith, R. C., Maroko, A., & Hopper, K. (2020). Menstruation and homelessness: Challenges faced living in shelters and on the street in New York City. Health & Place, 66(102431). https://doi.org/10.1016/j.healthplace.2020.102431

United Nations Human Rights. (n.d.). Sexual and reproductive health and rights. Office of the United Nations High Commissioner for Human Rights.

https://www.ohchr.org/en/issues/women/wrgs/pages/healthrights.aspx.

United Nations Population Fund. (n.d.). Sexual & reproductive health. United Nations Population Fund. https://www.unfpa.org/sexual-reproductive-health.

The University of British Columbia. (2019, November 5). Birth control options out of reach for many low-income women. UBC News.

https://news.ubc.ca/2019/11/05/birth-control-options-out-of-reach-for-many-low-income-women/.

Vora, S. (2020). The Realities of Period Poverty: How Homelessness Shapes Women's Lived

Experiences of Menstruation. The Palgrave Handbook of Critical Menstruation Studies, 31–47. https://doi.org/10.1007/978-981-15-0614-7_4

Weiss-Wolf, J. (2020). U.S. Policymaking to Address Menstruation: Advancing an Equity Agenda. The Palgrave Handbook of Critical Menstruation Studies, 539–549. https://doi.org/10.1007/978-981-15-0614-7_41

Wenzel, S. L., Andersen, R. M., Gifford, D. S., & Gelberg, L. (2001). Homeless Women's Gynecological Symptoms and Use of Medical Care. Journal of Health Care for the Poor and Underserved, 12(3), 323–341. https://doi.org/10.1353/hpu.2010.0797

Chapter 9

Aldridge, R. W., Story, A., Hwang, S. W., Nordentoft, M., Luchenski, S. A., Hartwell, G., Tweed, E. J., Lewer, D., Vittal Katikireddi, S., & Hayward, A. C. (2018). Morbidity and mortality in homeless individuals, prisoners, sex workers, and individuals with substance use disorders in high-income countries: a systematic review and meta-analysis. The Lancet, 391(10117), 241–250. https://doi.org/10.1016/S0140-6736(17)31869-X

Baggett, T. P., Liauw, S. S., & Hwang, S. W. (2018). Cardiovascular Disease and Homelessness. Journal of the American College of Cardiology, 71(22), 2585–2597. https://doi.org/10.1016/j.jacc.2018.02.077

Gilmer, C., & Buccieri, K. (2020). Homeless Patients Associate Clinician Bias With Suboptimal Care for Mental Illness, Addictions, and Chronic Pain. Journal of Primary Care & Community Health, 1–7. https://doi.org/10.1177/2150132720910289

Grewal, E., Campbell, R., Booth, G. L., Hwang, S., Mcbrien, K. A., & Campbell, D. J. (2020). 36 - Diabetes Management and Homelessness: Understanding Barriers Using Concept Mapping...Diabetes Canada/Canadian Society of Endocrinology and Metabolism (CSEM) Virtual Professional Conference 2020. Canadian Journal of Diabetes, 44(7), S17. https://doi.org/10.1016/j.jcjd.2020.08.042

Homeless Hub. Chronic Illnesses/Diseases and Mortality. https://www.homelesshub.ca/about-homelessness/health/chronic-illnessesdiseases-and-mortality

Institute of Medicine (U.S.). Committee on Health Care for Homeless People. (1988). Homelessness, health, and human needs. National Academy Press. https://doi.org/10.17226/1092.

Jones, A. A., Gicas, K. M., Seyedin, S., Willi, T. S., Leonova, O., Vila-Rodriguez, F., Procyshyn, R. M., Smith, G. N., Schmitt, T. A., Vertinsky, A. T., Buchanan, T., Rauscher, A., Lang, D. J., MacEwan, G. W., Lima, V. D., Montaner, J. S. G., Panenka, W. J., Barr, A. M., Thornton, A. E., & Honer, W. G. (2020). Associations of substance use, psychosis, and mortality among people living in precarious housing or homelessness: A longitudinal, community-based study in Vancouver, Canada. PLoS Medicine, 17(7), 1–24. https://doi.org/10.1371/journal.pmed.1003172

Merdsoy, L., Lambert, S., & Sherman, J. (2020). Perceptions, needs and preferences of chronic disease self-management support among men experiencing homelessness in Montreal. Health Expectations, 23(6), 1420–1430. https://doi.org/10.1111/hex.13106

Nikoo, N., Motamed, M., Nikoo, M. A., Neilson, E., Saddicha, S., & Krausz, M. (2015). Chronic Physical Health Conditions among Homeless. Journal of Health Disparities Research & Practice, 8(1), 81–97. http://digitalscholarship.unlv.edu/jhdrp/

Patten, S. B. (2017). Homelessness and mental health. The Canadian Journal of Psychiatry / La Revue Canadienne de Psychiatrie, 62(7), 440–441. https://doi.org/10.1177/0706743717711423

South Riverdale Community Health Centre. (2019, August 6). Chronic disease and homelessness. https://www.srchc.ca/news/chronic-disease-and-homelessness/

Chapter 10

Cheng, T., Wood, E., Feng, C., Mathias, S., Montaner, J., Kerr, T., & DeBeck, K. (2013). Transitions into and out of homelessness among street-involved youth in a Canadian setting. Health & Place, 23, 122–127. https://doi.org/10.1016/j.healthplace.2013.06.003

Doré-Gauthier, V., Côté, H., Jutras-Aswad, D., Ouellet-Plamondon, C., & Abdel-Baki, A. (2019). How to help homeless youth suffering from first episode psychosis and substance use disorders? The creation of a new intensive outreach intervention team. Psychiatry Research, 273, 603–612. https://doi.org/10.1016/j.psychres.2019.01.076

Ecker, J., Aubry, T., & Sylvestre, J. (2020). Pathways Into Homelessness Among LGBTQ2S

Adults. Journal of Homosexuality, 67(11), 1625–1643.

https://doi.org/10.1080/00918369.2019.1600902

Gomez, R., Thompson, S. J., & Barczyk, A. N. (2010). Factors Associated with Substance Use Among Homeless Young Adults. Substance Abuse, 31(1), 24–34.

https://doi.org/10.1080/08897070903442566

Grinman, M. N., Chiu, S., Redelmeier, D. A., Levinson, W., Kiss, A., Tolomiczenko, G., Cowan, L., & Hwang, S. W. (2010). Drug problems among homeless individuals in Toronto, Canada: prevalence, drugs of choice, and relation to health status. BMC Public Health, 10(1), 94–94. https://doi.org/10.1186/1471-2458-10-94

Groton, D. B., & Radey, M. (2019). Social networks of unaccompanied women experiencing homelessness. Journal of Community Psychology, 47(1), 34–48.

https://doi.org/10.1002/jcop.22097

Hull, M. (2020). How Homelessness Drives LGBTQ+ Addiction. The Recovery Village Drug and Alcohol Rehab. Retrieved 15 July 2021, from

https://www.therecoveryvillage.com/drug-addiction/related-topics/homelessness-lgbtq-addiction/#:~:text=Of%20The%20Recovery%20Village's%20survey,nor%20seeking%20treatment%20for%20addiction.

Kidd, S., Thistle, J., Beaulieu, T., O'Grady, B., & Gaetz, S. (2019). A national study of Indigenous youth homelessness in Canada. Public Health (London), 176, 163–171.

https://doi.org/10.1016/j.puhe.2018.06.012

Lautieri, A. (2021). Addiction Among The Homeless Population | Sunrise House. American Addiction Centers Sunrise House. Retrieved 12 July 2021, from

https://sunrisehouse.com/addiction-demographics/homeless-population/.

Murray, K., & Hampton, D. (2021). Homelessness and Addiction. Addiction Center. Retrieved 15 July 2021, from https://www.addictioncenter.com/addiction/homelessness/.

Pankratz, E. D., & Pankratz, N. (2007). Substance Use: Pathways to homelessness? Or a way of adapting to street life? Visions (Vancouver), 4(1), 9–.

Quayum, S., Hunter, P., Rivier, J., Cooper, I., & Baker, N. (2021). Report on addiction, substance use and homelessness. Government of Canada. Retrieved 14 July 2021, from https://www.canada.ca/en/employment-social-development/programs/homelessness/publcations-bulletins/report-addiction.html.

Schütz, C. G. (2016). Homelessness and Addiction: Causes, Consequences and Interventions. Current Treatment Options in Psychiatry, 3(3), 306–313. https://doi.org/10.1007/s40501-016-0090-9

Thomas, N., & Menih, H. (2021). Negotiating Multiple Stigmas: Substance Use in the Lives of Women Experiencing Homelessness. International Journal of Mental Health and Addiction. https://doi.org/10.1007/s11469-021-00560-9

Victor, J., Shouting, M., DeGroot, C., Vonkeman, L., Mark Brave, R., & Hunt, R.(2019). I'taamohkanoohsin (everyone comes together): (Re)connecting Indigenous people experiencing homelessness and substance misuse to Blackfoot ways of knowing. International Journal of Indigenous Health, 14(1), 42–59. https://doi.org/10.32799/ijih.v14i1.31939

Chapter 11

CAMH. (2019, October 7). Study by CAMH and St. Michael's Hospital shows Housing First program significantly reduces homelessness over long term. CAMH. https://www.camh.ca/en/camh-news-and-stories/camh-and-st-michael-study-on-homelessness.

City of Toronto. (2020, October 14). COVID-19 response for people experiencing homelessness. https://www.toronto.ca/news/city-of-toronto-covid-19-response-for-people-experiencing-homelessness/

Diamant, A., Swanson, K., Casanova, M., Magana, R., & Boyce, E. (2011, May). Improving utilization of medical care and health for chronically homeless adults with housing. In JOURNAL OF GENERAL INTERNAL MEDICINE (Vol. 26, pp. S342-S342). 233 SPRING ST, NEW YORK, NY 10013 USA: SPRINGER.

Fennario T., (2020, May 1) .Montreal applauded for opening facility for homeless, but critics say easier testing needed. APTN News. https://www.aptnnews.ca/national-news/montreal-applauded-for-opening-facility-for-homeless-but-critics-say-easier-testing-needed/

Formosa, E.A., Kishimoto, V., Orchanian-Cheff, A. et al. Emergency department interventions for homelessness: a systematic review. Can J Emerg Med 23, 111–122 (2021). https://doi-org.myaccess.library.utoronto.ca/10.1007/s43678-020-00008-4

Gaetz, S., Schwan, K., Redman, M., French, D., & Dej, E. (2018). The Roadmap for the Prevention of Youth Homelessness - Executive Summary. A. Buchnea (Ed.). Homeless Hub. https://www.homelesshub.ca/sites/default/files/attachments/YPRexecsummary.pdf

Gibson, V. (2021, January 12). Toronto shelter system records deadliest year on record, with 74 deaths in 2020. thestar.com. https://www.thestar.com/news/gta/2021/01/12/toronto-shelter-system-records-deadliest-year-on-record-with-74-deaths-in-2020.html.

McCormack, R. P., & DeMuth, M. (2016, June). Feasibility of initiating treatment for alcohol use disorders in the emergency department. In ALCOHOLISM-CLINICAL AND EXPERIMENTAL RESEARCH (Vol. 40, pp. 165A-165A). 111 RIVER ST, HOBOKEN 07030-5774, NJ USA: WILEY-BLACKWELL.

Ontario Agency for Health Protection and Promotion (Public Health Ontario). (2021) Health protection actions for people experiencing homelessness during the COVID-19 pandemic. https://www.publichealthontario.ca/-/media/documents/ncov/he/2021/02/covid-19-homelessness-environmental-scan.pdf?la=en

Sandberg J., (2020, August 5). Supporting First Nations citizens experiencing homelessness: MKO pleased to provide funding to YWCA Thompson. Manitoba Keewatinowi Okimakanak Inc. https://mkonation.com/supporting-first-nations-citizens-experiencing-homelessness-mko-pleased-to-provide-funding-to-ywca-thompson/

Richmond R., Stacey M., (2020, October 23) New homelessness strategy in London starts with Indigenous understanding. London Free Press. https://lfpress.com/news/local-news/new-homelessness-strategy-in-london-starts-with-indigenous-understanding

www.ingramcontent.com/pod-product-compliance
Lightning Source LLC
Chambersburg PA
CBHW022107160426
43198CB00008B/383